THE BETTER IN YOU

Let's contribute towards
the betterment of the
world together

ABHISHEK SEN GUPTA

BLUEROSE PUBLISHERS
India | U.K.

Copyright © Abhishek Sen Gupta 2025

All rights reserved by author. No part of this publication may be reproduced, stored in a retrieval system or transmitted in any form or by any means, electronic, mechanical, photocopying, recording or otherwise, without the prior permission of the author. Although every precaution has been taken to verify the accuracy of the information contained herein, the publisher assume no responsibility for any errors or omissions. No liability is assumed for damages that may result from the use of information contained within.

BlueRose Publishers takes no responsibility for any damages, losses, or liabilities that may arise from the use or misuse of the information, products, or services provided in this publication.

For permissions requests or inquiries regarding this publication, please contact:

BLUEROSE PUBLISHERS
www.BlueRoseONE.com
info@bluerosepublishers.com
+91 8882 898 898
+4407342408967

ISBN: 978-93-6783-827-3

Cover design: Daksh, Aniket Sengupta & Priyanka Sengupta
Typesetting: Tanya Raj Upadhyay

First Edition: January 2025

OM GURUVE NAMAH

DEDICATED TO

TO my father Mr. A.K. SENGUPTA & my mother Mrs. JUTHIKA SENGUPTA, for the love and exemplary upbringing they have given me.

TO my wife EKTA, for her unwavering support through all the ups and downs.

TO my both the sons VIHAAN & VIVAAN, who are constant sources of inspiration.

ACKNOWLEDGEMENT

I shall be grateful to PRIYANKA & ANIKET (my sister in law and my brother), for graciously designing the cover page

I sincerely thank all my teachers and mentors for their invaluable guidance throughout my journey

My heartfelt thanks to BLUE ROSE PUBLISHERS, for all the support and ensuring the book was published on time.

NOTE FROM THE AUTHOR

The very last chapter of this book (*Chapter No. 43. I QUIT*), was the first idea that I had in my mind while I started writing. Of course, as you go through the entire book, and reach that last chapter, its context and meaning will become clearer.

We all contribute in some or the other way. But when we do it with an awareness, its fecund. My purpose as a writer, was always to make this book accessible to everyone...who can contribute towards the progress in and around him or her. By available to everyone, I always mean, it should be understood to a teenager, who is growing up and to an experienced person, who has weathered life's challenges. So, this book is for everyone. Now, contribution towards progress can only happen, when we become better from wherever we stand today. This book aims to help readers to understand life in a simple way. This simple way shall further help, to implement simple things in life and gradually grow. Growth starts with improving self and change begins within

THINGS AROUND US ONLY CHANGE, WHEN WE CHANGE OURSELVES.....

As you read the chapters and understand what all things can really help you to grow and become better.

TABLE OF CONTENTS

CHAPTER-1 SELF TALK- THE BRIDGE TO DESTINY .. 1

CHAPTER-2. WHAT YOU SAY & HOW YOU SAY 10

CHAPTER-3 HOW TO HANDLE SHORT OF WORDS 19

CHAPTER-4 HOW TO AVOID- ATTARCTION OF DISTRACTION 24

CHAPTER-5 LOOK FOR PEOPLE, WHO LOOK FOR YOU 32

CHAPTER-6 KEY TO PERFORM- THE SELECTED WAYS 37

CHAPTER-7 ANGER- USE IT AS A TOOL 42

CHAPTER-8 "ME" VS "WE" 48

CHAPTER-9 SELF-CONFIDENCE.... *WILL ALWAYS BE YOUR WAY* 53

CHAPTER-10 KNOW HOW TO SELECT YOUR MENTOR 61

CHAPTER-11 ACCEPT YOUR SHORT COMING 66

CHAPTER-12 FORGIVE & FORGET 73

CHAPTER-13 BELIEF VS FAITH 79

CHAPTER-14 ABC & AUC 83

CHAPTER-15 WHY PROVE A POINT.... ALWAYS 87

CHAPTER-16 EXCUSES.... THE BIGGEST TROUBLE 91

- CHAPTER-17 TAKE IT EASY....WITH SIMPLICITY 95
- CHAPTER-18 KNOW YOUR PURPOSE 100
- CHAPTER-19 ACTION VS WORDS 105
- CHAPTER-20 DO...WHAT WE ARE SUPPOSED TO DO 108
- CHAPTER-21 GOOD THINGS VS RIGHT THINGS .. 113
- CHAPTER-22 ATTRACTING THE RIGHT THINGS IN LIFE 115
- CHAPTER-23 CHECK YOUR RUSH 118
- CHAPTER-24 ASPIRATION VS GREED 121
- CHAPTER-25 OPINION MATTERS 123
- CHAPTER-26 LESS IS MORE 126
- CHAPTER-27 LAST EVENING, YESTERDAY ENDED 129
- CHAPTER-28 EVERY CRISIS IS AN OPPORTUNITY 132
- CHAPTER-29 DEADLINE MATTERS 135
- CHAPTER-30 BALANCING WORK LIFE 138
- CHAPTER-31 GREAT VS GOOD 141
- CHAPTER-32 EVERYTHING HAPPENS FOR A REASON 145
- CHAPTER-33 PRESENT IS THE REFLECTION OF THE FUTURE 148
- CHAPTER-34 HUMILIATION HAS A PURPOSE 151

CHAPTER-35 DISCUSSION FOR ARGUMENT OR SOLUTION- CHOICE IS OURS 155

CHAPTER-36 EXPECTATIONS- CAN BE THE REASON FOR DISAPPOINTMENT 158

CHAPTER-37 PAUSE- THE DIMOND RULE 162

CHAPTER-38 F O C U S 166

CHAPTER-39 TOO MUCH 171

CHAPTER-40 LET GO 174

CHAPTER-41 THINKING LATERALLY 178

CHAPTER-42 UNPLUGGED 183

CHAPTER-43 I-QUIT 187

CHAPTER-1
SELF TALK- THE BRIDGE TO DESTINY

Talking to self is one of the most cherished liberties that every individual has. I am certain, you would agree as a reader. We often hear people say, "I am under so much stress these days" or something like, "I don't know, why am I the centre for all problems? Perhaps I am the only one who suffers, every time". These are very common lines, which people use and what could be the purpose for them to do so? Sometimes, it is just a purpose to gain sympathy while at times it is due to what people must have gone through at certain phase in life. This looks more of sympathy or support. The mindset becomes ingrained, influenced by experiences and the people around us.

If you see, we often assume that our thoughts and words are fleeting or inconsequential at times. We really do not know the outcome of what we say. What we say to others, or, talk to self, essentially plans our future. It rather builds our destiny, if I put it more concretely.

This is actually very simple to understand. As you go down the read, you shall cross over some situational examples, where you would understand, what we speak and what we think, can have extreme effects in life and can even change the course of life. *It is what you think you speak and what you speak is what becomes your thinking.* Let me explain you how duly this process works. No, you do not have to be technically scientific to understand this, yet sensible, before you speak.

See, it all in fact starts to frame, when you start to think something. This thinking or thought, is, mostly momentary and is just a fluid. Suppose, I say "Oh, Ekta, what a dull day today....don't feel like doing anything, life seems jaded". Understand, the first thing what happens here is, a fleeting moment comes to my mind, when it has nothing to do. What does it claim here, a mode of rest or laziness. This idleness, is often labelled as "BORING" or unexciting, which is very different from resting mode. As I say, "I am bored", now what happens to Ekta in that case, is a very interesting observation. Ekta, by the way happens to be my better half and whenever something prolific, is expected out of me, she steadily manages the driver seat and that too, she would sit behind me and guide.

So let's come back to Ekta here, where, to my said statement, she would have two possibilities. The *FIRST ONE* She doesn't get much interested and possibly agrees to me with an unhearing ear, when her squeezing nose along with her head nods up and down twice, not so slowly. Then definitely, now we both together, make that day, finally a boring day. The *SECOND ONE* here she looks at me, with scrunch eyebrows, and disagrees to whatever I said. Instead, she speaks out- " Is it so? I least agree to that. Let's do something together...hum...ok, let's go out for a drive". She speaks with a possibility and an excitement.

To both of her reactions my mind will also produce some actions here. Remember my statement- I said it is boring. This is already into self-acceptance of monotony, which is fix and not in quest of any change. Therefore, to the second situation, if I even agree to go out, which possibly I will, with the kind of persuasive approach Ekta would apply on me, the denial would be out of question. Though, going out wont tickle my happy harmones. My mind will seek for dullness from my body in resonance.

Ok, just taking the statement to a different boat of thoughts that is sailing. If, I would have said- "I am at a rest mode today", instead of BORING, things would have completely seen different sights at the shore. Understand, it was a moment, which made me feel that I have nothing to do. Most of us think, " Nothing To Do" means UNEXCITING. There lies the difference. "Nothing To Do" is simply "Nothing to do". It is just a state of relax, where, either one has completed a task or is going to begin another one. Whereas, saying this as boring, changes every perception towards non-productiveness. When you have nothing to do, its actually when you can start to think what is to be done next. There you find an occasion to do something, which can be very big, possibly for which you have been dreaming for long time. There is something to be done, when there is nothing to do. This is where a self talk can take you to, where you start thinking, the bigger self of yours coming into play.

Therefore, if we rightly understand, this self talk, which has certain ramifications, as per its practice. Once our thinking results into speech, which further converts into action, then there has to be an outcome. Thus, whatever we talk to self or others has to be well thought. Ideally, successful people, always do right and positive self talks, which keeps them motivated even in huge dump of challenges and that is how they are differentiated folks.

Let us take up some good examples here, to understand how should we do self talking. Prior to that, one thing you have to believe, whatever you say or think, will be making your future. Hence, *thinking -> speaking -> actions-> results*, you have to always keep in mind and understand it has to be the other way even. That is *results -> actions -> speaking -> thinking*. Once you have this 360-degree assessment, there you start to understand your own self and you outclass your past.

Suppose that, tomorrow morning you get up and say- " *Oh! God, today I am going to have a tough day, as I have a lot of things to address. Its seriously bothering as the day would end very late today. I am really worried; how would I plan things? Cant find a solution even*". This is well understood that you have a challenge at hand and you don't seem to be prepared to handle. With the above mindset, the chance of getting prepared becomes even minimal. Even if you get ready, solutions would be far behind from whatever you had expected it to be. Your, output won't be 100% towards win with this mind set. The words, you used here was, *'tough'*, *'bothering'*, *'worried'*, *'no solution'*. We used all possible means not to succeed towards our day's goal.

Now, let us change this somewhat towards a different mindset, you get up in the morning and say- " *Good morning God, thank you for giving me another day. You are so good that, you give me work to be addressed every day. I am so thankful. You take care of me and my family by giving me some work so that I have a respect in the society. You make me capable, and because of that, I can plan better. I request you to give me work everyday, so that I can do my bit in this world.* Check the words you used here. *'Thank you','good','respect in society','planning better','solutions oriented', 'positive aspect'*. When you use these words, whatever tough situations you may be in, you will put your best foot forward towards your duties and possibility of success and satisfaction becomes assertive.

Lets us further take up another instance related to work only. This is few years back. My good friend, Chandra, was out of work for some time. He used to work for a garment retail company. Due to some challenges within the company level, he lost his job. He was in touch with me during the search period. Whenever, he would talk to me, he would say, "Abhishek, I pray to God everyday that I get a job, somehow I need it badly." The anxiety was pretty obvious. He had to take care of his instalments, loans etc. Interestingly, this was not the first time that he had lost his job. Not that, he had any integrity issue, but, yes he could be an average performer, which most of us are. So, I happen to ask him, "Every time when you are out of your job, you pray to God to give you a job, and, God has been kind enough to provide it till now. If I may ask you, what do you really pray, whenever you have a job in hand". To this, the answer, that I got, was something very common. Chandra said, "You know when ever, I get a job, I pray, that - this time I must not lose it, else, I would land up into problems again." This was where the loop was. Of course, Chandra had seen the grey patches very frequently in his life, still he needed to come out of the loop of getting the job and losing it. What was happening, is, every time, he had a fear of losing the job, so his prayers were to save it, rather than focusing on performance. He never ever had talked to self, regarding his capabilities. I was thinking about him, how to change his loop and fear, which was not letting him move ahead. With a profound thought, I first advised him that, whatever, he thought and spoke to self, was his biggest challenge. I advised, "Even though, you might not find an immediate solution, still there is nothing you lose in trying out this statement. You should say to yourself every day, God I have got a job by your grace, now, I will perform here, learn every day and grow with my work. Most importantly, I am here to stay for long time". To perform, one needs to be ready with confidence, he was somehow missing that. Getting a job or an interview call, at times can be a destiny, but, the work, were to be done by us. Surprisingly, Chandra joined as an executive few years ago to a new job and now, he is managing a team of people. His team is very fond of him and they really speak very high of his leadership abilities. Most importantly, Chandra has not changed any company in last few years and has grown here. Now, he even tells his team to do positive self-talk, for whatever may be the situation in life.

With my next case in place, you will understand it better. Rita's parents, time and again keep saying, my child is not doing good in terms to health. Every time I take her out she falls ill. Rita is a 6 years old very sweet little girl, stay in my neighbourhood. Now, Rita also knows, that if she goes for any outing, she is bound to fall ill. She speaks to herself, I will again fall ill, if I go out. If we do a minor tweaking, and as Rita's parents, we say "Rita, you have started developing, better immunity as you are growing. Even if you fall ill, you fight and recover quickly. You are a fighter, and what strong mindset you show up dear. I am sure, next time when you go out, you will be fine."

Now, what happens to this girl? Firstly, she would start to believe that she is not ill and she is a fighter. As she is growing, her immunity is getting stronger, and she is confident of staying healthy. This self talk will change her for future endeavours as well.

We must ask our children to talk positive and look at the better side of life always. Tell them, yes, life would throw away challenges every time, but, with right mindset, right self talk and right actions, you will always get the best results. Remember, a child will listen to this but would follow his parents. Therefore, this should be practiced by us before we ask our children to do so.

To add to this, in case and whenever you have a financial crunch in life, don't say that " I don't have enough money with me, I am worried how would I survive, how would I pay off my loans, school fees etc." Agreed, you do not have as per the situation you are in. Still start saying, " I have my finances in abundance, things are really getting sorted, money seems to increase. God, you have been giving me in plenty. Keep giving me, and allow me to help the needy. You have given me everything in abundance." Now, tell me, those who look to do charity, how can they go short on funds.

Things can go wrong, and when we say wrong to self, we never can come out of the wrong situations. Understand, the situation, can be out of our hands many times, its how we talk to self and what mindset we keep during tough times makes us a different personality. So talk to self very cautiously with an optimistic mind, even if you are against the tides of life. This builds your destiny.

Remember: As what you think, is what you speak, and, so shall you become.

CHAPTER-2.
WHAT YOU SAY & HOW YOU SAY .....
MAKES OR BREAKS THE BETTER IN YOU

With my previous chapter, I emphasized on the understanding on how YOU can flourish, by doing just the right talking to self. Now, when you talk to yourself, it will have an impact on one's own self, but, most importantly, what you talk to others, can *make or break the better in YOU.* Here you will find whatever we think and speak, has its impacts not only at you but also those around you.

As they say, "**YOU ARE AS GOOD AS YOUR THOUGHTS**".

Question comes, how do others know your thoughts?? Yes, when you say, what you say, it is then, people start to know you. This is when the connection is developed. The gravity of the connection, depends upon, the way you have shared your talk.

The Power Of Words

" *thinking -> speaking -> actions> results* " I have already shared the concept it in my last chapter. You see, there are people, who become quick friends to strangers in no time. There are people who bring joy, and are loved. Everybody wants to be in their company. The reason is simple, they understand the person and accordingly they present their own selves. The thought process they have is quite clear, " I need to be loved, and respected, so I shall love and respect".

Take my friend Amit Dixit, for example. Hailing from Lucknow, the "City of Nawabs" in India. You see, these Lucknowites, have great flair in their dialect. They would always have this proper sweetness, with a mix of wit and humour, when they speak. So, Amit was always a star of the party, and due to his way of talking to others, he was super demanding. In fact, at times, we used to get envy of him, that how does he manage so many friends at one point of time. I am still to see someone in my purlieu, who has ever had a tiff with Amit. Most interestingly, Amit's first childhood friend, knows his most recent professional friend. The other possession what Amit has is, all his friends are from different backgrounds of work, creed or culture. Still, Amit manages to get them to connect with each other and for that he creates a common pliable platform, for everyone to be comfortable. What is so different about Amit here is, his thought towards friendship is very sorted and apparent. He believes in making friends, so his ***thinking -> speaking -> actions-> results*** compliments each other.

Clear Communication Is The Key

Often, what we speak, is misunderstood because we fail to articulate our thoughts clearly. Our thinking is much faster than our speech. At times, what we think and what we speak gets de-linked. This happens, when our mind is preoccupied with other things.

An Example Of Misinterpretation

In my office, one of my colleagues, often put things or talks about certain matters, where he refers to the subject saying "him" "they "or "her", instead of taking the relevant names. When he does this, people listening to him gets disconnected in his conversation. I recall an interesting incident- once this colleague of mine was working at his work station, when he received a telephonic call from one of our existing clients. They had a talk for almost 7-10 mins, where the listeners could make out that, both had some disconnect in their understanding and the discussion somewhat showed a disagreement. Now, interestingly, when both of them were over with the call, then my colleague, who seemed annoyed, spoke the following things to us (the team). My colleague said, "**THIS** person, says that **HIS PERSON** will not do the payments, until **THEY** share the outstanding sheet with his company." Now, the entire group was just clueless. **THIS** person, **HIS PERSON, THEY**..... were very hard to understand. There was a silence for some time, then finally my colleague understood, that whatever he spoke, he missed out to mention the subjects for the same, hence the entire objective of communication was lost.

This sentences could have been this way " *Mr.George* (instead of **THIS** person),says that *his accountant* (instead of **HIS PERSON**),will not do the payments, until *XYZ GROUP OF COMPANIES* (instead of **THEY**) shares the outstanding sheet with his company." Every time, we speak, we must speak with a clear idea, which is clearly understood by other. This is a classic example of not being clear, for what we want to share, or where the possible subject is in our mind but, not clearly put while communicating . So always, think before you SPEAK.

Many a times, what you think and speak can even be misinterpreted. This challenge generally comes across, when we mix up the medium of communications. I shall explain you what are the various medium of communications as we go further. Understand, if these medium of communications are mixed, or used wrongly, then there can be some serious damages to any relationships be it personal or business. I recall an incident, which would make this entire understanding much clearer..... It was one of those Indian summers of May, when the blistering sun had ruled the day and the temperature was hovering around 42 degrees. This was a Saturday, and I was enjoying the weekend. The sun, generally sets around 7:15 pm during summers in the northern India, just to give a bit of relief from the day's heat. That is when, I sometimes take a slow small stroll in my balcony and I was doing the same today as well.

Just then my phone rang, and it was one of my business associates, with whom I was talking after around six months. Generally when I walk and talk, I prefer to put in my ear buds as such I do not have to carry the phone all the way while talking. We started the talk with sharing greetings and well-being of each other, as most of us prefer to do. This gentleman had watched some of my motivational videos recently in YouTube and was congratulating me for what he had watched. On that, I shared my gesture of thanks. As we moved ahead with the talk, and I kept my leisurely walk continued, he proposed me a business plan, which I was sure, that I cannot do. I said on a stern and firm voice, "Sir, if you ask me to do this, then in that case I will raise my hand". To this, surprisingly, I realized, that I had raised both my hands, and, I presumed I was talking to the gentleman who was physically present in front of me. On the other side of the phone, there was a complete silence all of a sudden. I asked, " hello sir, are you there", and the gentleman said, " yes", and he sounded confused and asked, "why would you raise hands on me, you don't seem to be such a rude person". He paused and then laughed. I felt so sorry for the entire misunderstanding of thoughts that had taken place. My raising of both hands was understood to me, that, the proposal offered, would not be possible for me to do. Whereas, the gentleman's understanding was, my raising hand meant hitting or harming him.

Though, the talk was laughed out by both of us, but I really felt bad about this. Then again, no one hits someone, for any opportunity or business proposal being offered. Though this misunderstanding was on a lighter note, still, many of us suffer when we mix these medium of communications. It is also, true, that while talking no human can keep it close to perfection every time.

Speech is meant to be like that only. The natural flow of thoughts along with expressions, will have blemishes and perfections both. If this is so, then what is the worry all about? Actually there is no worry at all. It is just how we better ourselves, in whatever we do and my efforts is to get everyone better with certain mechanism towards communications. With this, let me take you to what you say and how it is said, depends on two understandings. First is the medium of communications and the next one is the variations of expressions. These both understandings can be simplified in the types of communications we use. This would further break down to an understanding of what we communicate, and, how we do it, while using the right medium with right expressions. Today the world is changing rapidly in terms to technology. The fist of future holds everything technically in its palm. So the communications also majorly depends in the technical sources available to us. The social media plays an important role here. I segregate the medium of communications into three segments.

1. ORAL COMMUNICATION
2. WRITTEN COMMUNICATION
3. EXPRESSIVE WRITTEN COMMUNICATION

I presume, who so ever is reading this book, must be having a certain and a sure understanding for oral and written communication. These communications have their own strengths and weaknesses. As long as, we know how to use these communications, it does wonders for us. The problem occurs when we mix the medium of communications.

Any speaker if you see, becomes successful, if the preparation towards his speech is done thoroughly, and then the delivery of speech if done with energy, rhythm, humour and articulation makes the speaker acceptable to the audience. Similarly, when a writer, wants to pen down the thoughts, and understands the readers mind, then only the writer is well accepted by the readers. So, assume, when a successful speaker wants to write something, or, a renowned writer wants to become speaker. Both of them are very much doable and many successful people have done this with style. Still, the way a speaker, presents his speech on stage has to be very different when he wants to writes something. Same goes for the writer as well. In both the cases, the audience who is a listener at one point and a reader at the other, vary in their mode of mindset while receiving the information. Majority of the times, we think that communication is just passing information. Whereas, any communication stands incomplete unless and until the information is well received by the receiver (listener or the reader).

Oral and written communications are very much in familiarity to us, as these are often used by us. Whereas, *expressive written communication* has been a newly born child towards mode of communication. This is a way of communication, which has been there due to mix of medium of communication. This birth has been possible because of the technology. This is mostly used in social media.

If I talk for *expressive written communications*, then today this is regularly being used while floating messages or through the medium where we send messages. Yes, I am talking of SMS. SMS is known as Short Message Service and some of us would surely know it. This form is just used for information purpose, as the name itself suggests. The challenge occurs when we become too expressive and use this platform as an explanatory platform. Our mind is very quick to grab, grasp and act. The emotional quotient is the dominance factor, so, that is the reason it always takes things into its control. Due to this EQ factor, we pattern our behaviour. The happiness, or the anger or may be any state of mind, is always reflected in our behaviour. Now, when we try and get these expressive emotions in short messages, imagine what happens. We feel, that the reader, would understand the message, which has come out of sender's emotions. Whereas, the reader, who so ever is reading it, could have different understanding as he might have some other emotions or mindset while reading. Now, what was supposed to be understood, can be misunderstood and then the interpretation of the message which is downloaded goes into a different direction.

Conclusion

Therefore, what is to be communicated verbally, should be done verbally. Similarly, we need to understand when we write something, it must be written, with the consideration that how the reader is going to read it and what he would perceive out of that. Mixing of things can really make our communications ineffective and unimportant. Effective communication builds connections, fosters trust and ensures mutual understanding.

Remember: what you say and how you say can only be better, if we understand the medium of communications.

CHAPTER-3
HOW TO HANDLE SHORT OF WORDS

Speaking is a natural process to humans. Then again, it becomes a challenge to many of us, whenever speaking is under the umbrella of performance pressure. It is a free-flowing activity, if it is not refereed, observed or questioned. Whenever the talk is under any scrutiny, the challenge of SHORT OF WORDS are confronted.

You see, most of us don't even realize when we have these short of words. Let us first understand, what are short of words? This would vary from person to person. This never bothers any individual unless and until, the person comes across any forum where he or she is asked to speak. Majorly, any impromptu meetings or presentations, where an individual is asked to deliver, here people come across short of words. People often think, how long am I going to speak for, or, what would the listeners think, if I get stuck in between my speech. Whenever, there is a comparison along with performance, there the individual face this situation. They might well have compensated their talk or speech through certain **FILLERS**, but, much to their dismay, the satisfaction after speech might have been missed out.

Talking about "FILLERS", now, what are "FILLERS"??

Fillers are the repeating words or interjections that we keep using to fill instead of the right word. This happens with many of us, and interesting part is, we do not even realize this, while we speak. Like many people use, "**I mean**" too many times when they speak. This shows that whatever one is speaking, is not confident enough and is into an explanation mode. We must have heard some people use too much of "**you know**" in their speech. So, when one uses "you know "many times, it truly reflects a certain assurance being demanded by the speaker from the listeners. There are many more known fillers, which most of us as individuals keep using and it becomes a tag to the speaker, which people talk about.

This challenge starts at a very tender age in most of us. At that point of time, many of us are not given the solution to rectify it and as we grow up, it becomes a frequent problem and results into lack of confidence in individuals. The best part is, if this challenge is met at any point of time in life, it can accurately and perfectly be rectified.

As and when we counter these challenges, we can have the following simple solutions:

Avoid Repeating Words: We will have to find out a way where we get away with the repeating words. Now as the challenge is known, we should find a simple and easy solution, which is convenient to implement. We need to apply a basic rule of sorting. By sorting I mean, being more organized in our speech. During any speech, we always try and engage the listener. For that, we need to get them into an agreeing mode or a yes mode. What we are speaking, we must presume the listener is there to listen to. So, if we use words like YES, WELL, RIGHT(as asking gesture) or some similar kind of words at regular intervals during your speech, then the speech gets automatically sorted and is very much accepted. So, one sentence can have a "YES", in an asking posture, where people who are listening to you would generally agree. Similarly, usage of "RIGHT" or "WELL" also gets the listener in the agreeing mode with the speaker. If one uses these variety in the speech, the speaker sounds very certain and definite, and is well accepted by the listeners. This variety while talking, shows maturity in the speaker, and the speaker if even forgets certain words, he or she, finely gets away or overcomes short of words problem here.

Slow Down: Everyone has a different pace in their speech. We often get tempted to speak fast. The mind is faster than the speech, so the thought which flows, must be synchronized properly with the speech. If we keep a slow but uniform pace while talking, things are easy to put as well as understand. By slowly, I do not mean a long pause after every word. It must be in a flow, which would give the speaker a room to think and then take the thought rightly with speech, which further will help the listener to understand as well. So when you talk slowly, the challenge of not recalling a word is actually tackled in a sophisticated way. The speaker looks much sorted and gives a sense of being an intellect.

Use Simple Words: As a natural tendency, while speaking, we often think of impressing the listener. There is nothing wrong with this. In fact, at times the speaker thinks that, unless and until the listener is impressed, the share of talk given by the speaker is not accepted by the listener. This piece seems complicated at both the end. If one speaks some ornamental words, which requires very high knowledge to understand, then the speaker is limiting his or her talk to just a selective group of people. Some words which are very tough to understand, at times makes the listener lose interest. Speech should be as simple as water. If you hear, some of the world best speakers, you will find an instant connect. They try and speak very simple words, which are easy to understand and absorb. Also, from the speaker's point, easy and simple words, gives the speech a natural flow and the challenge to short of words which is easily taken care of.

Embrace Pauses: When you talk slowly, this gives you a natural tendency to manage your short of words problem in your speech. Now, a pausing, shows the speaker much refined and composed. This pause benefits the speaker in many ways. It works as a blessing, when the speaker comes across the short of word challenge. As I mentioned earlier, mind is faster than speech, so, while pausing, we actually do nothing but recall the right word that we might have missed while in our flow of talk.

Keep Sentences Short: Too long when we talk, would be prone to mistakes and the interest of the listener also gets impacted. The flow of talk should be very even. One who is listening, should never deviate. Therefore, it is recommended, that we must use small but clear sentences, while talking. The sentence that we frame, must be very specific to our topic. As a speaker, we often tend to flow with the talk, and, there, many a times the disconnect takes place. This detachment in speech, when we realize and think of coming back to our prepared topic, we often miss out in words. So, framing small sentence is generally a master stroke, to counter short of words.

With all these in the approach, and a regular talking practice with self, can surely help any individual to come over this challenge of short of words.

Remember : What one speaks, is not for the sake of just speaking, but, for the sake of making the listener understand about what one spoke.

CHAPTER-4
HOW TO AVOID- ATTARCTION OF DISTRACTION

For most of us, success is everything. More than the attainment of success, it's the journey, that leaves an impact and is cherished. This cherishing is often realized when we have completed the journey and have tasted success. During the journey, we often get unforeseen turmoil, the path is often fraught with obstacles, where the journey becomes a pain and few of us leave it in between instead of completing it. None of us want any challenge during journey, still they come knowingly or unknowingly.

Let us understand this with an example. Imagine a train is running with its supreme pace over the track and suddenly a derailment happens.... why did this happen?? or What could be the reason??

It could be anything. Now, I may ask, what could have been the reason...without even knowing we would say our part. This would take us to a certain debate, like some would say the track was faulty, while some would say the driver must have over raced, or there could be any conspiracy to derail the train.

Here, as a reader, if you observe, I started with quoting success, then I put up an example of a train getting derailed and further I stated, the reasons. The entire flow had certain distractions from where we started. Similarly, distractions can derail us from our intended paths.

What Is Distraction

This attraction of distraction is something that no one wants but the world is full of amazing and attracting opportunities. Consequently, it is so hard to neglect. Before we take it ahead, we must know what distraction all is about. Distraction is an attraction, towards something, which is strong enough to disturb the right amount of attentiveness, that is required to do a task or work that one has taken up. Now what happens when one gets distracted. Yes, at the first go, the importance or the essence of the work taken in hand, is lost. The journey, that one had begun, to gain something, gets dissolved midway somewhere. Everyone, who dreams of achieving their goal in life comes across this situation. 95% leave them midway somewhere. Only those, who are determined against all probabilities, make it to the finishing line. These group of people are very less in number, and they are the people who are a successful bunch.

I feel that we all can come over this challenge. See, the problem is not about getting distracted, which some of us might get over. Then again, if the comeback is not in time, then we miss out on the larger aspects. It has harder repercussions, on any individual who lose their path, may be due to any reason in the middle of their journey. The suffering big time. There's resentment, agitation, mental imbalance , distress and many more of those.

Realisation

Distraction is somewhat different from any other problems of life. As far as, problems are concerned, we realize them only when they come to our life. With distraction, it is not so. With distractions, we will only come to know, when it has already settled within us, or, sometimes years after it has gone, post it drifted us from our goal way back in the day.

So, do we think that distractions are natural. Surely, if you ask me, it is a big YES. It's very natural and each one of us goes through it. Therefore, if its natural, then why do we need to be careful or cautious about this. Rather, why do we even need to think to stop this. In fact, let us know several ways to handle it. The elimination is inevitable. To handle this, here are few points that would help you to stick to whatever you are doing and come back if in case you get distracted and how you handle distractions.

1. Listen to everyone but follow your plan:

    Many a times, in life we often plan to do something, apart from our regular work that we have been doing. For example, someone wants to start any new business. This could be short term or long term, irrespective of any ambition. Now, if someone has a plan for any business and have zeroed in to start, there would be people, friends or associates, who become super active and start to advise in many ways. Some of them would encourage and some would create a doubt. Now, as the business, is already at a naive stage, and the person who is starting, is doing from scratch. Considering that he or she has no experience of business in the past, has a high possibility to get drifted from the path that one had drawn. This is one of the most common distractions that people face. At times, the drift comes from close family associates even.

Solution: The best way to handle this situation, is simple. Just, listen to your heart. Yes, I mean, just listen to your heart. Go by the plan, that you have. No plan is too long, to manifest. Times and situation will keep changing, but, what you have dreamt of, should remain constant and concrete. Thus, listening to others, is always good, doing what you need to do to reach your dream, should be done. So, avoiding distraction is out of question, but here, we learn to handle it. One must have a strong reason and ready to walk down the path, where distractions will also give way, for the dream to take place.

2. Back to basics:

   This is the easiest path that one can take at any given time. Majority of people get confused when they get away from their goal. They try out many new things, which might or might not be fruitful. Then again Back To Basic, is the most sorted mantra that can plug in the things back to normal. No doubt, it is always tiring to go back to basics especially when one has travelled far ahead in the journey towards the goal. There is truly no alternative to hard work. This is how, repeating the work again and again, proves one to rectify and not to repeat the mistakes that possibly one must have made earlier. To stay consistent and persistent, throughout, is something that many are not able to maintain. Then again, goal taken in hand by any body, has to be reached, and everyone is allowed to attain, who so ever has a dream. When one has countered distraction, then back to basic will always help to get them back to consistency and persistency. Honestly mentioning, when I started writing this book, from where I had left, last time, I used to find a unique challenge of mindset being different every time. Therefore, to maintain my flow, I had to go back to the beginning of every chapter from where I started. By doing this, I could align my thought back to action. This is the simplest yet overlooked approach, to come back into action, whenever one gets distracted. If we see, the successful people, or some great sportsperson, they always preached and practice this art of back to basic whenever they lose track.

3. Mind your own business: The rude that these words look, if implemented to self, it yields remarkable results. Sadly, whenever we have used this line of statement, it has been used for others and have not fetched us appreciation rather have ensured that we made a critic out of ourselves.

By minding one's own business, I first of first mean, that it must apply on myself and not to anybody else. The world is full of competition and extremely skilled people. There would be people who could be better than us in many aspects. There would be certain times, when many of us would try to reach towards a common goal. At this point of time, distraction has a very different and strong weapon to attack with. It shakes our belief level and damages our confidence. For example, if we go back to our childhood, many of us were good athletes.

So, during any track event, we must have observed, the contemporary who was sharing the neighbouring track, at times gave a steep fight or would have been even better. Now, if one thinks this, before the race, then the race is lost even before it starts. Here the attraction of distraction, shakes up the confidence.

The best way to avoid this is to focus on self or mind one's own business. It's obvious, if one has gone for the participation of the race, then that person must have practiced sincerely, consistently and persistently. Therefore, the faith within shall prevail. Moreover, what one can do is, perform and perform with vigour. Who knows, if it's your day, then you might even beat the world's best. So, chances and possibility are always there. Just we need to mind our own business.

4. Planning, Evaluating & Routine: Certainly, this part manages the most of self-control and helps us keep away from distraction. What we plan, how we plan, is what matters in anything and everything that we task out. Planning can be phase wise, as it is subjected and related to the small goals being attended before the larger one. When we plan short term, we evaluate the result. This becomes more productive when we make self- evaluation a habit, at every step of the journey being done. Now, even if we get distracted at any point, the process of self-

evaluation becomes a valuable check point. Planning should always be by a checklist, that one needs to mark in self-evaluation. This checklist must be cross verified in a routine manner. Now, if routine is firmed as a habit and religiously practiced, then, even if you get distracted, the routine will give an alarm and make you come back from where you got distracted.

So that whenever you drifted, go back to your plan of work and check what all have you finished and what all are remaining. Therefore, planning, making routine check a habit and self-evaluating, is a great way to counter distraction.

There must be many ways to come out of any situation. I am trying to help you as a reader with some basic tools, which if applied, can be of great help to reach and fulfil your dreams.

What shimmers takes the attention but not always the heart.

Remember: Attention divided is purpose lost. Therefore, purpose is everything. Stay true to your goals and success will follow.

CHAPTER-5
LOOK FOR PEOPLE, WHO LOOK FOR YOU

Modern interiors, glossy workstations, crafted walls and a fresh pool of people. This was the new office of an apparel brand that I had joined in Gurgaon (Now Gurugram) in India. Someone has rightly said "Don't try to follow trends, rather create them". These words were embodied by this trendy company. I was rejoicing this new charming atmosphere.

They specialized in mainly T-Shirts and a mix of smart casual wear. I was hired to develop business in modern and channel trade. In those days, channel trade, or, I should call it as channel sales, were driven by state agents and distributors in India. To reach out directly to any garment shopkeeper, in a specific market of a particular city, was always a tough task for any brand. Moreover, brand had a different vision and it had to reach all possible markets. Now, if there are certain specialized people, who can take your business to the right target customers, then things at brand's end got easier.

I had been into apparel and retail sales throughout my professional career, so therefore, I was here to drive and expand. I was apt ready mentally to take up this new challenge. My considerable experience and learning allowed me to take this exposure as I had known few big and renowned distributors and agents to become the channel partners. They were well known to all the shopkeepers in their respective states, and the shopkeepers had high regards for them as well.

Confidence And The Unexpected

My perspective was clear, and I was pretty sure that I will crack the business with these partners. The kind of rapport that I shared in the past with them, made me even more confident. Generally, you start the deal with, the person you know the best in the list and can vouch for. Whenever, you will be in need, then these group of people will be there to help you. I too had this mindset and started the discussion with almost being sure to get my first business. As soon as I called one of them, and told him about my new assignment, he was so excited to hear the news and congratulated me on the same. As the conversation proceeded, I got even more sure that my first channel partner was almost appointed. I shall just be doing the on boarding paper works and get him going. To my dismay, with my sanguinity of mindset, came the unwanted denial. This is what, I had least expected and was not at all prepared for. When my first channel partner denied, trust me, I got really surprised and was a bit worried. He was the best in his market and if he would have been ready, I would have had a smooth journey. Then again, if everything is as per our wish, things will be so cool, no. This was disheartening but I reminded myself of the wise words of famous poet

Harivansh Rai Bachchan "*Man ka ho toh achcha hai....naa ho toh aur bhi achcha hai...kyon ki who Isshwar ki iichcha hoti hai*", means, " If things are as per our wish, its good....if it not so, then even better....because that is Almighty's wish". I had been preaching it, and these precious lines, have given my creative self a chance to move ahead, whenever I got stuck.

Reevaluating My Approach

Nevertheless....to prove your credentials, you need to move on, whatever may be the challenges. With this, I approached few more, who were equally good, and had similar trade experience. I was not able to crack any single deal. Something, somewhere, was not going the way it should have gone. Time was knocking, and my owners, gave me an expression, which had a smile, that showed, that they were still confident, but, their eyebrows going up, surely showed an anxiety too. Then I thought of figuring out and listing down the reasons for rejections. I needed to understand the limitations, at both ends. I figured out few important things. The people, I was approaching, had already built up a substantial business over the years. The appetite to grow, in life, for them, was very selective. Therefore, time that would be given to any new project, from their end, would matter. I found, it was more of a rejection process rather than a selection process. So, the demands, the channel partners kept in terms to commercials, were unjustified. The pay outs were more what they demanded, post we worked out on our economics. Ours was a new company, it would have required a good amount of leg work, at the initial phase. So, the energy that would be required, to be productive, was also of a considerable amount. Rest of them, I found contended with their existing business.

Finding The Right

I realized, I was approaching the wrong people. They, might have gone big over the time, they might be the super heroes of their trade, they might be the known names in the market, but one question remained strong....Do they want to grow with me ???

I needed to look for someone who was looking for me. In other words, I needed to do some leg work myself, rather than expecting someone else to do it for me. How clear the things are, that if you are required to grow in life, it's you only who must do his or her piece of work. I started approaching people, who were smaller distributors, but were holding good credentials. Few of them I approached, and even liked. As, I was in the process of finalizing one, I came across a person, who approached me to be a partner with this new company. This gentleman was working for some apparel company himself and wanted to start something of his own. He had a good name as an employee in the market and was ready to take on the charge. For this, he had to leave his on-going job, through which he was drawing a good salary. His intent, to leave his job and take a risk to start a business, spoke a lot about this gentleman. As I had known him, so his integrity was not under any such scrutiny. Moreover, he was willing to provide the necessary deposits and agreeing to close the paperwork as per the company guidelines. I had to pass on this message to my promoters. They were new themselves, so they could relate to the situation, that was similar. With this, finally, we started of our new trade of channel sales in this company.

The Lesson

It was understood, we need to look for people who were looking for us. We went on to appoint many more distributors, agents and retailers, who were willing to grow together. Just to mention, today most of them are doing good business. Its all about giving opportunity to the person, who wants to make it big in life. The zeal to walk through and the hunger to grow makes them a different identity. Wherever we are today in life, we must have been given that first opportunity, may be knowingly or unknowingly. We were looking for them who were also looking for us.

Remember : what you seek, seeks you as well. So look for them and keep looking until you find one, who is also ready to walk the path with you. There you will make a great connection.

CHAPTER-6
KEY TO PERFORM- THE SELECTED WAYS

Adam, was out an out a key person for business in his company, that he was working with. His PR skills and a positive mindset along with his dedication was something that people used to talk about in his organization. Even the newly appointed, use to look up to him, and the management was also very happy with his performance. Adam's, role was primarily client servicing. Many times, his bosses even felt that his sincerity and the way he came up with the solutions towards the problems of his clients, were commendable. Possibly client servicing was naturally to his instincts. As per his qualifications, he had a graduation degree in hotel management and further he pursued HR. Now he was handling clients and was generating sales revenue for his company. To most of us, who would deep dig into his qualifications, it would look very different. The qualifications he had, were in absolute contrast to what he was doing now.

The same was not the case with his company. His higher management was rather thinking he was versatile and can execute any additional responsibilities. Adam was a productive guy, and was a level three, which is of a middle management role. By now, he had spent five years in this company. What happens with time is, people seldom remember your past achievements, degrees, qualifications, and the right skill sets, rather they look at the present. So, same was the situation with Adam. His past specializations, spoke about his people skills. His hotel management degrees and then HR, helped him to understand people, therefore, client servicing, helped him to be productive. He was surely a people's person. Adam, was a people's person, was not really known to he himself, as his core quality. Therefore, the same was not understood by the stake holders. Rather, he was read as a performer, who was excellent in sales. To do sales, or any other thing, once needs a special skill set. This skill set can be anything, like anticipating abilities, people skills, profound knowledge, experience over the time spent.

Friends, there is always a big difference between a driving role and an executional role. Most of the time, people with authority take decisions for people, for whom they work. Adam's versatility was of handling people. And his company's higher management, were thinking that he had skills to deliver other duties, which needed technical and foundational grip of knowledge. So, as Adam was into middle management, he was more into execution rather than driving things. To drive, anything one must have sufficient knowledge of the relevant subject or the domain that one has to take on or which he is supposed to drive. By, looking at his performance, he was added with another responsibility of internal coordination with HR and client finance handling. Now, managing the internal team and at the same time meet the targets of sales, had their own constraints. Therefore, with time, his performance deteriorated. Someone has so truly said, if you try to catch two rabbits, you will end up catching none.

This is what happens to most of us, when given additional executional responsibility in lieu of some lucrative offers. If we are not prepared enough to take on the responsibility, we shall surely make mistakes and our performance will go down.

So to understand the key to keep performing, we must focus on the following things:

CHOICE OF WORK: As we go ahead in our career, we start getting many lucrative offers. It is not that you should let them go. The only thing which everyone should know is about making the right choice. If the work attracts you, and you are sure to handle it, go for it. Ensure that you have relevant information and proper knowledge of the work. The skill set can be developed, but without right knowledge, the skills won't be much effective. Therefore, right choice along with right knowledge, can make you productive and keep your performance good.

QUANTUM OF WORK: How true, one should not take, more than what one can chew. Piling up work just for the sake of taking, will always have a negative impact on our performance. Many of us tend to do this, when we think, that taking of more work will make one secured in any organization. But, actually it happens the other way. When we take more work, and, are made to do justice on the same, with due timelines into considerations, we can always fall. We must know what is the amount of work which we can deliver, rather than taking more and not delivering. Never shy away from saying a NO, but humbly. Sensible people shall always appreciate. If you say a NO, say it always gracefully and humbly.

VISION & PLANNING: A right performer, should always be able to envisage. Foreseeing the probable and then planning things accordingly is one of the most classic traits of any performer. This should be very well understood, with an example of making of a dream house. Most of us have this dream to build our own house. When we plan a house, we visualize it. This visualization is then shared with the architect and then the planning of layouts, drawings, elevations etc. are drafted on paper. This blueprint is followed by a sincere approach of planning. In between, if some of the things do not go as per plan, its ok. At least, the base plan is ready to start the things and accordingly, some tweaking can be done if required. Whenever you get stuck or distract in between, you should always go back to your initial vision that you had seen. This is the power of visualization. You just need to envisage. Going back to things, helps to rectify. This you can call as follow up of your vision.

Remember : Performance is an act to presenting. To perform well, focus on what you can control- your preparation, actions and your mindset.

CHAPTER-7
ANGER- USE IT AS A TOOL

"Anger begins with folly, and ends in repentance ".

This famous quote, given by the great philosopher Pythagoras seems so correct, when we deeply think over it. Anger is surely a part of everyone and is a natural emotion. One of the most unwanted expressions, which each and everyone would be least happy to express.

Getting angry, and expressing it however, are two very different things. We tend to express anger towards those we perceive weaker or dependent on us. On the contrary, those who are superior to us or whom we rely upon, there we try to control our expressions of anger, so that things do not go awry. For example, an employee might endure scolding from a boss, without retaliation, knowing their promotion depends on that relationship. This is somewhere good and complimenting, where we control our anger and show a true sense of maturity. But, as soon as we come out, we often spill the anger to someone, who have absolutely no link with the situation. Like, we might land up showing the anger to our subordinates or to our immediate family members and even to our kids. Just think over, when we reach home after our days' work, our kids and family wait for us. They have much to speak about their day, how it went by. They have, some possibly very important things to share, which might not be important for us, but for kids, their sharing is precious, and we must give it an ear. Knowingly or unknowingly, we carry our anger to our home. When we take them out there, things really go very wrong.

Understanding Anger

We must be a person of character. We must know how to control our angry expressions. To control anger, we must realize or try to know anger. When we know it, we should try to control it. We need to use anger as a tool. let's see, if we can use anger as a tool.

First, let's discuss, how we can know our anger. It's simple. As I have stated above, getting angry and expressing it are two different things. Now, there are two very self-important possessions. **Respect** and **Ego**. So, if our respect is hurt we feel bad and if our ego is hurt, we generally get angry. Respect generally gets tarnished, when someone insults our cadre. First, we feel bad, and then if our position is at the receiver's end, we try and accommodate it with just feeling bad, unless and until it reaches extreme level of our tolerance. When it reaches the extreme, we can't control and there is an even possibility that we might get angry.

On the other side, if our ego is hurt, then the paradigm shift from feeling bad to getting angry is extremely quick.

The shift from expression of feeling bad to expression of anger, is almost impossible to determine. Now, here we have known two facts that is *feeling bad* and *anger*, how and when they can affect us. If we consider the respect angle first, someone who does not respect, the best thing is to move away from that person or if you cant get away, try and avoid direct contacts as much as possible. To be true, many a times, moving away, does not become possible, but, if you have known the matter, you must develop your matured instinct to handle it by not paying attention or be silent. If someone doesn't give us our due respect and we keep expecting the same, then it shall be in vein. One must work with people or be in that company of people, where there is respect, else, it is always better to leave that association, where there is no respect. Feeling bad or getting angry will only harm self.

Next, point is ego. This is absolutely a point within, which is majorly about I, Me and Myself. The more you give important to self, more than anything else, you will always land up making more foes than friends. Respecting self and giving importance are separate. Respecting self will always make one respect others and make and individual more humble, whereas, too much self- importance, puts a cover on the eyes, due to which the self of the person misleads one from the understanding of right or wrong. Ego is therefore, the most common factors which gives rise to any form of anger. We all know, our ego, and if we know it, and, still promote it, then anger will always rule our mind. So, if one has ego, and wants to work on it, then again simple steps if taken, things can be better gradually. To work on.... Say to self, *"I shall be foolish and the biggest foolish of the world, if I cant work on my ego. Only foolish people have ego, and I am not foolish. Life is all about adding people to your life. Loving and caring them. I am there to understand people, help them and give a smile to every face I meet, through any medium."* This affirmation if done for twenty-one days in the morning, then anyone can find a substantial change in self-behaviour. By the virtue of this activity, one will always find, respect is growing in plenty. If respect is gained, just be humble and thank God.

Now, when we have known the reasons to get angry, we must know to control it as well. The simple method of controlling would be, to foresee the repercussions. If you have read it till here, I believe you have well connected with the thought process and are intelligent enough to understand life and work towards better. This also means, as a reader, you a looking to change for the better always through every and any medium of learning. The right person would always think before he or she acts. If I may just pen down, what all are the results of anger. As per every mind and state of anger, on whom and where it is coming out, the outcome can be very harsh and extreme. As I mention extreme, then many relationships and even life have been at the cost of small angers issues.

It has been noticed that when we are angry, we do two very reactive things:

One is, we start talking to self in anger when alone and create that situation in mind, due to which our anger emotion grows up. This happens when the person is not available in front of us, on whom the anger has broken out.

Next is, whenever we are angry with any person and he is with us, we express it with our hand and body movement. This is not only to hit, but also, we move our limbs under anger expressions. These observations can surely speak of knowing the signs of anger and again once the point is known we must restrict self from doing this. At the second instant, where one moves the limbs especially hands, the person, should hold one hand with the other and in some time, the person who is angry, will realize that, he or she has started controlling the anger and is proacting to the situation.

Using Anger As. A Tool

If one has known the factors of anger and why to control it, then anger can be used as a tool. This tool makes one a better and a far better person every time, wherever one is standing at any given point of life. To use it as a tool one must elevate the self- thought process. This tool can be to improve self. When we try and control our anger, we develop patience, we develop more of self- control and understand balance of temperament. We develop humbleness, when we let go the situation of anger. We progress as a person who has the capacity to understand others and help others to control anger.

The process of self- healing starts here, and you get introduced to a better concept of life.....To forgive and forget.... And move on.

Remember : Anger when controlled, can lead to growth. When left unchecked, it leads to regret.

CHAPTER-8
"ME" VS "WE"

"ME" vs "WE", this distinction has been a critical component of human interaction. If you see both initial first letters, "M" and "W" they are mirror opposites- a symbolic representation of their contrasting meanings.

Many people, find it hard to acknowledge the contributions of others , if they are a part of any team. Specially if any individual has done the most of it, in spite of being a part of the team. This insecurity is with most of us, and that is fair, as many of us are not aware of the importance of "WE" in life.

The Fair Understanding

Few years ago, when I was working for a corporate, I had come across a situation, which gave me a lot of insight about the importance and the right understanding of "WE" in comparison to "ME". Before I take you through this event of my life, let me put an important note that "I", "ME", "MY", "MYSELF" all are from the same family, when it comes to express ME.

Getting back to the incident.... This was 2005, December winters in Delhi. I was with a multinational credit card company. We had been doing direct and corporate sales. The credit card being international, the terms and conditions in comparison to other national card companies, were on the tighter side of approvals, before we sold it to the customers. So, we had several team members under few responsible team leaders. Further, the team leaders reported to one General Manager. Thus, the hierarchy was lean and straight. The teams, under the leadership of team leaders always had an internal competition. There were good perky incentives, which every team would thrive for. Amongst all the teams, one of the team, used to always sell maximum cards and earn majority of the incentives every time. Somehow, initially, I did not have the fortune to be a part of that team. Being into sales, the pressure of selling was always high and whenever there is high pressure, the peace at work place gets effected. So, some team leaders were really hard task masters and if we say that out of carrot and stick theory, they were the people who opted for the stick to drive their respective teams. We had monthly reviews about the performances and accordingly the ratings were given to each team.

Once, in every six months there was a meet, with the Zonal Manager. This time, I was being introduced to this meeting first time since my joining. The presentations started at 9:30 am as scheduled. Every team started presenting their status of work. Most of the team leaders addressed and liked saying "MY TEAM" or "THE TEAM", whenever it was about the non-performance part. By non-performance, I mean where they had lagged in achieving the targets. As soon as there were some achievements, the leaders said WE or US or OUR TEAM. The stance suddenly changed. The energies while presenting was very different. Now, most of the team leaders were just following each-others way of presentation, or possibly this was the way they thought of covering their skin towards non-performance, by using THE TEAM OR MY TEAM, and the opposite i.e. WE or US came into the saying, anywhere there was an achievement. Then, the major observation came from the person, whose team performed most of the time. This gentleman, started, with WE. He stated a WE in everything he said. We performed as a team and acknowledged, why We missed as a team (if in case they missed out meeting the targets). He gave all the credits to his team for all achievements and stood strong for the things they missed by guarding his team. Finally, by late noon all the presentations ended. Then the General Manager was to share his understanding for the performance of the day. To this, the General Manager praised and appreciated the leader, whose team had performed consistently. He stated that the leader's approach was much appreciated, and the major difference was of all ownerships that he had taken in every thick and thin, by addressing a WE. This was a clear message for others to learn and take this message on a profound note.

You see, whenever we say ME or my team, this looks more of a self-proclaimed or self-possessed approach. The listener receives a perception of a person who has a lot of ego and with him a distance is to be maintained. Whenever it is about a team, it must be a WE always. Good and capable leaders do this bit in such a refined manner, that they develop more of a cohesive approach and a great bonding amongst and with their team.

Just imagine, a good soccer game, where one player performs extraordinarily and is the key player. He also happens to be the scorer, but the only challenge lies with him is he is not a team player as he does not pass the ball to his fellow players. The ME inside him does not allow him to do so. How long will this team perform? Will his teammates and coach want him to be a part of the team? Possibly no. There will be a rift and a certain downfall. Remember, every time, if there is a team, then the right leader should take the bunch together and should share the credits and take the debits rightly.

ME vs WE:

ME is always about an individual whereas, WE is about everyone or togetherness.

ME will limit whereas, WE shall expand.

ME doesn't allow you to share whereas, WE is all about sharing.

On the other side, ME has its own strength and one should know when to use it.

Now, if you really want to use ME and see the good side effects of this, then ME must be used for self-realization, self-improvement, self-motivation. The self-talk to be done is very important here. *"I will improve"*, *"this is my team "*, *" I am so grateful to have a team, I love my team ".* *" I will keep them motivated"* . *"I shall lead from the front, and take all debits and give all credits to my team rightly "* . These are few thoughts, where a deliberate ME has to be used, so the WE become more productive and strong.

Remember: A good leader takes ownership for everything and uses "WE" in place of "ME" to unite and inspire.

CHAPTER-9
SELF-CONFIDENCE....
WILL ALWAYS BE YOUR WAY

"Believe you can and you're halfway there" ...

some of us might have heard this famous quote by Theodore Roosevelt. How true they form, in making anyone so sturdy to achieve something, which many might not have imagined ever. This inner strength to seek and get what one wants, with the right ability, quality and judgement, is what self-confidence is all about. To an extent, each one of us are blessed with this quality. Few of us are fortunate enough to understand and majority of us are unaware of this universal strength which originates within. The success stories of inventions and discoveries done, the historic victories are all testaments to the unwavering self-belief of individuals who dared to dream.

Now, there are two major aspects towards self-confidence. The First one is, if we have it within, why do not we realize it? Now if we do realize it, why does it go away most of the times. The second thing is, if it goes away, how can we bring it back every time? This means, that, as a reader you need not to worry, whenever you lose confidence, after reading the below mentioned formula, you can always get it back.

Why We Lose Self- Confidence

I shall take this up with a personal example. You see, cricket as a sport, is a religion in India. This sport is very popular in every part of the country. People here, start playing this, at a very tender age. I attended a boarding school in Mussoorie. Mussoorie is a hill station in the Shivalik range and is the base of foothills of Himalayas in India. This place was mesmerizing, and the climate here, in this part of hills, has its own natural way to express itself.

Coming back to the story of cricket, cricket playing, in hills during those days, were subjected to the climate and could be played in limited months only. Unlike the plains, in India, where people could play it almost round the year. We had a good two months winter break in December and January. After our winter break, as we came back from vacations, in mid past February somewhere we would start playing. This would continue till May end. So the span for this classical sport was just 3-4 months. I truly enjoyed the sport. Was a left- handed batsman who could bowl a bit as well. As the duration was just 3-4 months and we could play it in weekends only, so, I always wanted to make the most of it, whenever the opportunity was there. We would play inter class and inter school matches. The competition was tough, as there were many children who, wanted to make it to the playing eleven, especially for the school team.

It was one of those years, when I was not batting good enough. I would have been in class 9th that year. They call it a bad patch in cricket. I was possibly going through my bad patch. I generally used to open the innings for my school as well as for my class. I wasn't performing good with the bat. Entire mind set had shaken up, it was no more from which position I would bat at, now it was either I played well, else, I should sit back at the pavilion and cheer up my team. When, you go through challenging times in life, then the margin to perform well, also shortens. Here, it is about the right mind set, and confidence, which sets you apart from others, when you perform with a limited resource. Now, as I said, I could bowl a bit, so I thought, to be in the team, I must try my every bit to perform and contribute to the other departments of the game. Therefore, I focused on my bowling and fielding. When you channelize your skills in certain directions, then, they result into achievements. As I started to focus on my bowling and fielding, my pressure to perform with the bat reduced, which eventually let me settle down first and then extract the better, in me, as an all-rounder.

At that point of life, I was just too young to understand myself or the concreteness of realizing my self-confidence had worked or not. But it had worked and for this I thank my teacher and coach, who realized this potential in me. Later, I realized why my performance went down. The reason which I could figure out was, one of my school fellows was batting good, and I was worried on how could, he be so good. My position was not affected by his way of playing. Rather, it got effected because, I was losing my confidence due to wrong area where my focus was. The moment, I changed my playing field along with my mindset and focused to my skills, then things started to shape up good for me.

This is one of the principal reasons of losing confidence. Rather than improving self, we get effected by others and develop a complex of inferiority.

The Opinion Of Others

Next, reason of losing confidence is, when someone, whom we believe or trust, forms an opinion about us. This is troublesome. You see, many a times we go to people whom we have been looking up to for one or the other reasons in life. He or She is generally, can be anyone, either a mentor, or a family person, even can be a teacher, in fact anyone. Whenever, we take some big decisions in life, we go to them and ask if the decision taken is good to go ahead or not. At the first go, if we have taken any decision, it should be well thought and must have certain level of belief. This firm belief is reflection of our self-confidence. The moment we ask someone, it shows that the decision taken is unsure and there the person whom we ask, forms an opinion based on our past relationship, past performance and understanding. Also, possibly, the person whom we have asked, might not have full knowledge about the project, but still, will share his point of view based on your past, what he thinks about you.

Presume you have been working as a salesperson from a company, which sells pens. Consider yourself, as an average performer. Now, after a certain point of time in your life, you plan to start a business as a distributor for pens, who would supply the stocks to the shopkeepers. The confidence to do the business comes to you because you have seen this format of business for some time now and you have gathered experience for the same. You have also developed certain relationship with the retailers, and you have an expectation that if you service them as a distributor, at least 50% of your existing customers will support you.

Now, you decide to discuss this plan with your ex-colleague, with whom you were working long time ago, but you are still in touch. He is still working for some company and have reached a higher level in life. He remembers you as an ordinary sales person, who performed average while doing the job. Now, his opinion for you, would carry the image, that he had seen when you were working with him. Over the time, you might have grown, still there is possibility he would point out your weaknesses, which shall lower your confidence. Again, it is not necessary everyone, discourages. This example is specific for a particular situation as mentioned.

Therefore, it is always better, whenever you plan something, go by your instinct. Do not fear the failure. One never fails, if you succeed, then good, if you do not, even better, because you come up with some learning. Now when you do it again, then you are sure not to repeat the same mistakes, which you might have done earlier. If you treat your failures as learning, your confidence doubles up. You don't repeat the same mistakes again.

Rebuilding Self-Confidence

Losing of confidence is very natural to every human, but, gaining it back and then perform again, is what separates one from the crowd. I consider that there are these specific three things, which can always keep your confidence very high.

The first one is **SKILLS**. God has been supreme and has made all of us special in some or the other way. Its just that, we sometimes fathom it and sometimes we don't. If we understand our own self and our natural skills, along with our limitations and strengths, things become much easier in life. Some people are, super skilled and do good in multiple fields, but, if you have a single skill set and you are aware of that, then, you need not to look at others. Bruce Lee the karate legend once said.... " *I fear not the man who has practiced 10,000 kicks once, but I fear the man, who has practiced one kick 10000 times*".

The second one, is having **RETROACTIVE** approach in life. This is really one of the best tools, to boost your confidence, if in case you have been feeling low. If we see, we all have certain achievements in life. They are always there to make us feel good or make us special in our own eyes. These achievements, act as blessings, if we really consider them, and trust our own self. Self confidence is nothing but trusting our own self. What a fine quote Les Brown has given to the world, " *When life knocks you down, try to land on your back. Because, if you can look up, you can get up. Let your reason, get you back up.*"

The Third in my list is, consistent and persistent **PRACTICE**. Getting success is never an easy phenomenon. It takes years and years of focus and practice, if you are looking to achieve something in life. As I mentioned, if you have some specific skills, that will always give you an additional push to do something, but, skills without practice catches rust. By now, you must have understood, what is skill and why you need to do practice. As practice is an over the years dedication, and as you go ahead in life, this over the years statement, come up with different challenges at different stages in life. We are humans and the challenges many a times become so strong, that we tend to give up. Whenever we feel like giving up, we should always look back and get up and practice for whatever we look to achieve. The goal should be very clear. What we want and why we want...then confidence just becomes a part of yourself.

Remember: life is a blessing, and only thing that we can control is self, which we must control. So if you control self, all becomes under your control......... *Just you should know how to control self. Self-confidence will be always on your way.*

CHAPTER-10
KNOW HOW TO SELECT YOUR MENTOR

"KARMANYE VADHIKARASTE MA PHALESHU KADHACHANA, MA KARMPHALA HETUR BHURMATEY SANGOSTVA KARMANI". This means, you have the right to perform your duties but you are not entitled to the fruits of your actions. These lines in Sanskrit are from the famous religious book Bhagwat Gita, *Chapter-2, Verse-47*. This narrative framework of dialogue was told by Lord Krishna to Arjuna. Lord Krishna was the Mentor and the charioteer of Arjuna, on the battlefield of Kurukshetra. On the battlefield, Arjuna, was in a state of dilemma, whether to fight the battle or not, against his kinfolks. He could foresee the devastation, that the wrath would create. Then the Lord counselled Arjuna, to fight for this righteous war. This was his karma (duty) to participate in the battle, and which he must.

How tough it must have been for Arjuna, to take up this decision. On one side he had his extended family and on the other side a mentor, who was guiding him to fight. Krishna also stated, " Arjun, you must fight, if you win this battle, you will get the kingdom, the dominion, the people, and whatnot. If you attain martyrdom, then you will come to me. So in both ways, if you see, you shall be benefitted".

This is what a mentor does. Guides, nurtures, polishes, prepares, and makes what you have not thought of even. Therefore, selecting the right mentor is very important.

The Comparison

Going back to the epic, Mahabharata, there were two different mentors, at the same point in time. Both of them had very different purposes to fulfil through their disciples. One was Lord Krishna, who was mentoring the *Pandavas*, we may call him the protagonist. The other mentor was Shakuni the maternal uncle of the *Kauravas*, we can call him the antagonist. We project them as protagonists or antagonists, because of the purpose they had. Krishna says, Life is an opportunity, utilize it, live it, and do your duties wholeheartedly. Whereas, Shakuni teaches a different version of life to his followers. Shakuni says, you are an opportunity, become an opportunist, take everything by every means, that seems possible. We see different ideologies, and we are good enough to understand, who is right amongst the both.

I believe there can be three possible situations to search a mentor.

1. MENTOR BY CHOICE
2. MENTOR BY FORCE
3. MENTOR'S CHOICE

1. **MENTOR BY CHOICE**

   When we find our mentors, we prefer to do it by the virtue of our selection and requirement of ours. We can choose from any given list. Sometimes, while doing so, we start looking at their personal aspects rather than considering their professional capacities. Let us understand this with an example. Suppose, you want a badminton coach for your child. You come across a coach, who has been coaching a good number of aspirants for some time. Somehow, you come to know, he has some personal family problems. Now you contemplate, will he be the right person for this possibility of coaching? Should I go along with the person? These considerations will not help you to take the right decisions. Therefore, whenever, we are finding a mentor by choice, we should always consider the mentor with his abilities. The past legacy that he holds in his field. This will always make our job easier.

2. **MENTOR BY FORCE**

   Here things become very different. The best example that comes to my mind is all about the tough bosses from corporate. Yes, some bosses are very hard taskmasters. These mentors are always by force. One might not even want to be under these people, but they have no choice. These mentors can actually exploit the abilities of the people, who work under them. As it is, one does not have many choices or can do much, so it's better to restrict yourself strictly professionally. The more you become personal, the more liberty you shall give the boss to exploit you. Nevertheless, it is up to us, how much we can learn from their experience. Then again, the right things have to be learned from these people. If these mentors don't put themselves as people's manager, then one of the finest things that, we should learn from them is to become considerate and good people managers.

3. MENTOR'S CHOICE

This one is very interesting. Here the mentor has a clear purpose to select his disciple.

The mentor is in the hunt for the right disciple. The mentor looks for a potential candidate, who can fulfil the objectives of the mentor. The best example is Chanakya. Also known as Kautilya. He was a teacher, tactician, author and minister of the Maurya Empire, (marked in ancient Indian history **375-283 BCE**). He selected his disciple Chandragupta Maurya, who rose to power as a great king. Chanakya, had played a very important role in the establishment of the

Maurya empire and also became the chief advisor. These mentors make their disciples great. This is what Krishna did to Arjuna as well. The purpose of these mentors are very clear. It is truly a destiny's call to have such great mentors, who select their people to do great things.

The most important thing is one must have a mentor, a coach, or a guru to grow in life. Whatever field we are in to, we must have someone, who can guide us. Every life needs a guide. Those people are fortunate who have had a mentor, or we may call them guide, teacher, coach, counsellor whatever we want to address them as.

Remember: Every life needs a guide.....and we must respect our Mentors....if we have one.

CHAPTER-11
ACCEPT YOUR SHORT COMING

" I am a human, and I fall and fail, I feel and I find, I also give up and cry, I have flaws and scars, as I am just a human and only a human".

Its life, and it's absolutely ok to falter. Life's a journey and we are here to travel the path of life. We may fall but must get up and get going. That is how life is meant to be. So classically if we may see, if you have to reach the rose, then the path is through thorns along the stem.

The Right Approach

Short coming is a part of each and every one of us. Many of us, make it the centre point of the life, and starts prioritizing and believing this. How we accept and deal with it, makes all the difference. There have been people, who have had extreme challenges in life, be it physically or mentally, but, they have done some extraordinary work, in spite of these challenges. I always, see a special example in this context to put though. Helen Keller, was one who could neither see nor hear. She had a permanent condition of being deaf and blind. This was not by birth to her. She came across a brain fever when she was very young and her age must have been 19 months then. Post that, she was a child who was reckless, violent and she could hardly communicate. She could have been easily declared a child who must need special care as she was not normal, like any other child. But then, when she was seven years old, she had her eureka moment. Where she discovered what she was meant to be and how she had to walk the path, which was much unknown. Post her discovery of self towards life, then there was never looking back.

Imagine, a child, in the 19th century, fighting with all spirits to make it a point towards survival, when there were very less facilities for everything unlike today. Still, she went on to write books, became a political activist, a lecturer and a much-sorted speaker. This is so much of an achievement, for someone, who had not heard the applauds ever, which must have been so encouraging for her, otherwise. Neither, she could see those inspirational faces, who must have looked up to her every time she made public appearances. Still, she went on and on just to do the purpose, and the purpose is keep doing your work, for what you are meant to. The column of expectations in her sheet of life, must have been so negligible in her mind. How could she do so much, I keep imagining, as most of us, look for something or the other to support the short comings. I believe, the only way to do so much, is to accept what and who we are. How much can we deliver, where can we improve, and how can we excel, by understanding self.

The Acceptance

This can only be possible, when we accept, who we are. What are our strengths and weaknesses. When we know ourselves better, we can always work on those concerned areas. The only big challenge comes, when we do not accept. We actually, as a human, most of the time, do not want to see the problems. Problems, if they stand tall, in front of us, we get worried or are fearful to face it. Remember, we can only win over any problem, when we face it. This face off, with any problem or challenge, gives us a hope to restore the things back in track. Now, why do we not want to have this face off, is because of certain short comings that we know we have and the problem lies in that area of our short coming.

The only possible way to counter this is to accept the short coming and work on that area. This will be clearer with an example. We possibly were best fighters when we were kids. Whatever we wanted to prove, we just focused and were among the noticeable children. I remember, such an event when I was 11 or 12 years old. As I have stated earlier, mine was a boarding school, so the area on which the school was built up, was huge. In our school, there was this wall of around 4 feet in height, which separated two sides, on way towards our classrooms. I had a short height, and short enough to climb that wall. All my friends would cross over, with ease. They just ran towards the wall, put their both palms and flied in style to the other side. I somehow, could not do it, even with good number of attempts. My friends would get an opportunity to pull my leg, over this. This short coming, of not crossing over, really bothered me.

As they say, what you want from the universe, universe ensures to give you, provided your ask is concrete and strong. My ask was concrete, and the way universe chose to grant me, is something, which I still remember. There were, some stray dogs which would often, come inside the premises. Because of hills in the surroundings, the dogs had some easy access to the compound. They were always in groups, and behaved very wild. In fact, they had bit, some students, in the school. School authorities were also trying to take due measures in this regard.

Then the eventful day came. Today, I was their selected prey. Now putting it to you, for reading, is very different, but that day.... as I remember, I still have good number of chills rolling down my spine. It was early morning, and I thought to take a stroll before the breakfast begins. As I was crossing this wall pathway, which was with the turn and downhill, I saw them standing. Initially, they did not do anything. Looking at them in a cluster, I stopped. I was alone and had no other choice but move back. Moving back was uphill. As soon as I started to do so, they began their share of chase, which was much faster than mine. They were at a distance tough, but, I was sure, that in a gap of few seconds, they would get hold of me, and I would have been all theirs. So, it was matter of just few seconds. Then all of a sudden, I saw that 4 feet mighty wall, standing as tall as it used to be. With no choice left, I thought, if not today then it is never again. I will anyhow, have to jump the other side of the wall. My two legs were doing their bit, as much as they could, but those four legs multiplied with five or could be six of them were just superfast. Now, I reached this wall, put my both palms and fully stretched and plunged....yes, I saw myself at the other side of the wall. I could feel the barks were just behind me. Today its seems so dramatic, but that day it was something, which I still am scared off. Ultimately, I did it, but the way it was done, should have been the last thing, I would have preferred.

This was a learning for me, when we are in the biggest of problems, our short coming, becomes our strength, we just need to accept it and work on the same. I could only jump that wall because, I was practicing doing so from some time before.

The most important part here, is to accept the short coming. You see, I have seen many kids these days, if they are told something, they should improve on, they would generally listen, and start to work in that regard. Provided, it is told to them in the right manner. But as we keep growing up, we develop a self-resistance, towards self-improvement. Some people whom I have met while counselling and mentoring in behavioural aspects, they say, that, many times, its embarrassing to accept the short coming. They fear, even if they accept, they become a talking point amongst their surroundings and circle. I believe it is just a perception.

First thing is, if I am improving, I am improving for my own self. It has got nothing to do with what others think. Next important understanding should be, we are always open to learn, so we should be always looking for correcting self, whenever and wherever required. It is very simple to understand, if someone is working for a multinational company, and has been promoted from an executive to a middle management level, then there must have been something good, that he or she must have done. Now, to reach ahead to a senior management level, from the middle management level, the person, has to do something, which he or she aspires for.

What brings you here, won't take you there.

To reach the higher aspiration, we got to work accordingly. As the aspiration is a self-generated approach, so to work on self and short coming, should also be a self-oriented thing. It has got nothing to do what others think. Successful people, just do it this way. There are people, in this world, who are disabled, but they still have made it big and beyond expectations. The classical Bharatanatyam dancer from India, Sudha Chandran, lost her leg in a road accident. Later with her courage and self-belief, she gained some mobility with the help of prosthetic foot. With rigorous practice and the will to come back, she performed many dancing shows in India and other countries. One of them, who overlooked his disability was Stephen Hawking. His disability and still going on to do his bit in the field of science, shows how ready he was for his duty. It is just about accepting yourself as you are and work on the areas that you should be working to better your life. Excuses and reasons, will always be there, but then the questions come....are you really looking at the excuses or the opportunities. The simple difference is.... *"why I should not be doing it"*, OR *"how can it be done"*, makes you a different person altogether.

Remember: Accept your weakness and celebrate your shortcomings, it will help you to become more stronger and overcome it gradually.

CHAPTER-12
FORGIVE & FORGET

A few days ago, I started reading this famous book - *Ikigai: "The Japanese secret to long and happy life"*. Even the title intrigued me, promising a sense of purpose towards life. I was so engrossed in this book, while reading, that few of the things were very clear from the first few pages itself.

If we talk about life, it has its share of challenges for each one of us. The formats and specifications of challenges may vary from one person to another. Truly, none of us have control on that. The more power we give to challenges or problems (as many of us call it problems), the powerful they become. Then again life cannot be just led with unhappiness, worries, jealousy, ego, revenge or something, that keeps bothering and hunting, which makes us away from people. Forgiving is divine and it takes a lot of understanding, compassion and courage. Whereas, forgetting is a instinctive human trait. When we mix both, it is a worthy combination, which we all should learn to do. Forgiving is easier said than done, but, if we learn the art to do so, then it is worth every ounce of effort. I know this firsthand. Learning to forgive has certainly brought an undeniable sense of serenity to my life. I have some great sharing in this regard, which I would like you to know as well.

A lesson In Forgiveness

It was those initial years of my career, when I used to work for an apparel company. The brand was renowned in India and people, who were working in this apparel company, used to take proud in the association. Those, were not a part, always dreamt to become one. "Someday, I must work in this organization", that was the thought. Same did I too feel. As they say, what you look for, looks for you in return. My destiny, somehow, decided to make me a part of this organization. I was just so proud and happy. It felt as if I now have differentiated myself from the rest of the crowd, in my field of expertise.

Being into sales and marketing, my job was always demanding, and I knew that I shall have to take this challenge. It was those, foggy chilled winters of January in India, when I first entered the office. The very first day, I was handed over a laptop, as my previous company, were still on planning stage. In sales, those days, laptop was not that mandatory for salespeople, though there were desktops. The gradual evolution towards technology, was taking place, and I was part of that progress. The feeling was wonderful. The mechanical world here was super supportive. I thought, I will have a great journey here. I was still to meet my immediate boss and the people I shall be working with. Little did I know, what was coming my way here.

My boss had been working here in this organization for quite some time, and he had taken few gradual promotions. There was a bit of favour that he got from his superior. This was very clear and evident. My boss lacked good human behavioural skill, and many people kept good distance from him.

Days started rolling in the calendar, and my work started. As the days went by, I realized that, he was more of into a bullying approach. He used to humiliate his subordinates in public. The sad part was this behaviour of his, was not known to the head office, and we were at the branch office. When you work, you will make mistakes, and that's how it is with everyone. Those, who work and take initiatives, only shall make mistakes, it is as simple as that. Now for every mistake, you will be up to some humiliation. People, fear humiliation the most. So, errors become very common, as the self-confidence, is lost. We must refrain our people from public humiliation, if we are a leader. This should not even be done to kids, as many parents do it unknowingly.

With me this was just exceeding day by day. The moment, I used to come to office I started having same fear every day. Somehow, when I went back to home after work, I used to feel low on my self-esteem. In fact, my wife, who was then very newly married to me, started noticing the change in behaviour. Believe me, I used to just feel so stressed. Which now, I realize, should have been tackled. Least expected out of me, I thought of leaving the organization, as the torture was unbearable. It was impacting my personal life. Had I continued there for some more time, my confidence and the urge to grow, would have been finished forever. This is very important for us, that, if something which is not working for us, we must take a call immediately. Many times, its not possible, but, unless and until we look for opportunities, we won't get them either.

Time has travelled, since that day and not much of interaction has happened with that person. Now, I realize, what all he has taught me. He has taught me to be a better person in life. Never to bully the people, who look up to you. Always take care and teach good things to your subordinates. Help them where ever possible. Overall, when you work with someone, remember, when they go back home, they should be happy with their family and must be taking about you, in good faith. I now thank God that I met him or the people, who had troubled me sometime somewhere. It is because of them, today I am a better person within. I have forgiven them for what they have done. This is the reason, if now when I meet, I should meet him with a better heart. My forgiving and forgetting approach, will make it easier for me to meet.

At the same time, I too seek forgiveness, every day, for the wrong I have done, or even I have hurt someone knowingly or unknowingly.

Why Forgive and Forget

Forgiving means healing self. God helps us to go through these rough patches at times, just to make us a better person. Its up to us, what we pick from our sufferings. Revenge or forgiveness. Both will certainly, have different paths. Similarly, both will have different climax. Forgiveness is possible every time and with everyone. Just you must settle your ego. Ego becomes the major problem, and then there are people, as we think, what will they think. People, in and around us, do not have much time, then forget things very easily. So let us value self.

Revenge is very subjective, you can only take it, when you have the opportunity to do so. Till the time, you have the opportunity, which is again conditional, you suffer and lose most of your precious time. With you, your family or your people, will suffer as well. Therefore, you will have to make the wise choice. What you want healing self or suffering unconditionally?

It is not always easy to do so, but, if we attempt, we can surely come close to it and become better. Matrix of understanding is simple, are we trying to change the world around us or should we be changing only self. We must change self, things around us will change automatically.

Remember: Forgiving is a gift you give to yourself. Make it a everyday practice when you go to bed. Seek for forgiveness, and prioritize not to repeat it. Then forgive them who did hurt you. You shall always sleep better.

CHAPTER-13
BELIEF VS FAITH

One of my mentors, once asked me- "Do you believe in me OR do you have faith in me". It was his much deliberate approach to put me to a litmus test. As expected, I was too new to handle this question. I stood blank and confused for some time and to keep up to my reputation, I said both. I thought that a statement which holds no ambiguity, should be good to go. My mentor smiled and after a pause he said, "When you go back today and ask yourself, what actually you should have". Since that day, till today as I pen down, I every time ask myself, what should have been the correct answer.

The Nice Comparison

The question is so simple, yet complicated, when one has to select the either of the two. To me, belief comes first followed by faith. To have faith in something, one must believe in that. What is belief- It is a state of mind, which one considers to be true and exist, and not necessarily it should have a proof. Like I believe in myself. So simple, statement this is, and most of us use it generously. It holds certain truth and exists within, and you cannot prove it to others. Whereas faith is something, that is strong enough a trust or confidence, on someone or something. To have faith in God, we must first believe in God. Many of us do say this, that we believe in God, but the factor comes, do we have faith in Him or not.

Belief does not require any evidence, so there is no scrutiny either. It is as good as stated. The thing that makes all the modification is faith. By faith I mean, whatever is the requisite has to be done.

I came across a fantastic story on belief and faith. This story made it very clear what was what. There was a father and a son. Son was around 7-8 years old. They were skilled acrobats, who used to perform feats on tightrope. Many call it tightrope walking. The father used to carry his son on his shoulder and walk from one end of the rope to other. To earn some bucks, he made it more enterprising. He was so skilled, that with his confidence, he used to walk from one end of a one-story building to other. This made him very popular in his city. There was certain flair of risk involved, but with his confidence, he made it look good every time.

One day while he was performing, he was a bit unwell. He told his son, "Today I should perform the feat alone, as I am unwell, I might lose out in my balance." To this his son said, "Father, will go together, and with me on your back, you will never lose the balance." This was the faith that he had in his father. So, they started the performance. Half down the way in the rope walking, the father seemed to lose focus, but his son said, "do not worry dad, I am with you. You would never let me fall".

They certainly made it to the other end of the rope successfully. The story doesn't end here. It has something more to it. There was rich man who was watching this show with his son, from his luxury car. After the show ended, this rich gentleman walked up to the skilled performer and praised his talent. This rich gentleman now started insisting him, if he could perform this once again as his son wanted to watch it once more. Though the rich man, was ready to pay him some good extra money, still, the performer resisted, as he was unwell, that day.

The rich man now started to insist more and was some how becoming commanding. The performer thought for a while and then said, " Sir, do you believe that I can perform this once again". The rich man said, "yes, why not", with a strong poise. To this the performer said, "you have faith, that if I carry the child, I shall be able to make it to the other end, as I am unwell". The rich man now could see some interest in the performer, and said, "yes, I have faith in you". Now the performer said, "there will be a small change in equation, instead of my child, I will like to carry your child this time." This was something, the rich man never ever expected. He was speechless, and there was silence for some time. There was a confirm belief but, the faith was missing.

This story made me understand the difference between the two. Faith and believe do go together, but, necessarily they might not superimpose each other. When we travel in a flight, we believe and hope that, we, would land safely. Question is...how much faith we have in the pilot who is flying the plane. Another classic example, that I put here, when we fly a child from our hands into the air to catch him or her again, they go up with a smile and they have faith in us that we shall hold them come what may. This is faith, or the trust, as we may call it.

If we believe in something, we will have to believe it to be true at the first go. This benefit of doubt has to be passed on. Then only the faith can be reinstated always and every time. Mind you, if faith is lost once, then, it is very hard to restore. The reason is simple, faith or trust is on someone or something, so it depends on others.

Remember: Always believe in yourself and this will develop the faith.

CHAPTER-14
ABC & AUC

We humans often tend to look what others are doing or how they have done, what they have done. We also seek inspirations out of them. Nothing wrong at all in that. Only thing here matters is, what they have done, how they must have done that. This "how", is very situational. By situational I mean, when the work was done before, they must have been done under different circumstances, that existed in those times. Now, the same "how" if needed to be done, will have entirely different requirements. Therefore, if the same success story is to be repeated, then, things should be as per current situation.

Very interesting short forms, which I had learnt few years ago. Since then, I have been trying to see things, that I do, should fall in either of the category, which they eventually fall. ABC means "AREA BEYOND CONTROL" & AUC means "AREA UNDER CONTROL".

The Understanding

This reminds me of Chanakya. Chanakya was an ancient Indian polymath. Who was a royal advisor, teacher, philosopher and author. This concept of ABC and AUC was made very much clear by him in those ancient times.

Once, he was with his disciples for an activity that was to be performed. During that activity, there came a situation, which required some individual tasks and some group tasks, to be done by the disciples. The tasks were not easy and required some serious involvement. Few students started debating or figuring out how this situation could be addressed. The confusion now was shaping up into a chaos. The debates and the commotions were not hidden from the teacher, who had purposely, given them this task. When he saw, things were not working out as it should have, Chanakya, called them and explained them how ABC and AUC are to be prioritized. He stated, work that you see, can be done easily, do it first. Once it is done, then take up the work, which requires others to help you.

How To Prioritize

One must know which work is to be done how. Firstly, we must consider, AUC (Area Under Control) . In any activity or situation, we must first sort out things, that is under control. The work that is doable and is under capacity of doing should be given the priority rather than ABC or (Area Beyond Control). ABC is very circumstantial. We can also say that its indirect to us. So, once AUC is done, then only we must consider ABC.

This situation is countered when we have multiple work to be addressed. Whenever, we are not able to prioritize our work, we waste good amount of time in decision making. As an outcome, none of them gets done properly and within time.

The question here is how to be more meticulous in understanding ABC and AUC. Sometimes, the work is pickup due to duress or force, which we do not want. This happens mainly because of wrong leadership. This leadership can be anywhere, it can be in office, it can be amongst friends and even inside family. We are not left with much of choice, at these junctions. Now, if we are caught here in ABC, then also, we must figure out, what is the area of AUC (at the micro level) in the given ABC (which will be the macro level). This is known as sorting. The more complicated is ABC, the better sorting we should do with AUC.

The best few ways to get things apportioned and be productive is, one must follow a routine pattern, for whatever one is doing. Routines benefits us in very many ways. It starts from our own self. The more disciplined we are in our daily life, the better classified we shall become. If we are a strict follower of routine in our life, and even if some ad hoc event comes, we can get them sorted by the routine approach. It is as simple as that, what we can do you should be done first, instead of wasting time, on what we can't do.

Let us get back to our child hood, and recollect the examination hall. Some of us might remember, during an exam, there were some sections of children, who got stuck up in solving one problem or question, which they had not understood properly. While trying to decode the unknown question, they missed out those easy questions, which they knew. On the other hand, few of the students always, did, what they were able to do first. Then they hovered into those questions which were not very clear to them at the beginning. This was the major difference, between good and average students. Routine always helps to plan things.

Remember: Always eat the low lying fruits first, and then climb the tree further.

CHAPTER-15
WHY PROVE A POINT.... ALWAYS

Somewhere I had read , when you try and establish your words with shout, command or noise, it shows that the reason that is being established is either weak or wrong or needs validation. Therefore, whatever is true, shall never be required to be proved. It is always a matter of time, truth shall prevail.

The Context

For example, if someone says, that physically you are not a human. Simple, if you can read this, you are a human. Now you do not need to prove that to anyone. This straight example looks weird, but then do you even bother to prove this? That means, what is true is true, and one must not waste energy in attesting it.

Sometimes, yes, if in case you need to prove something, and that is in concern with the legal aspect, then it is apparent that you must have evidence, to do so. The entire context is different in this case.

There has been a basic observation, that, whenever we try to prove any point, we force ourselves on others. This compelling, takes our voice always on the higher side. Whenever we are loud, we are generally not accepted by the listeners. Whenever we are not accepted as a listener, then, the entire purpose of proving goes in vain. So, what is lost, needs to be reckoned.

The Understanding

First, the self-energy is lost, followed by the goodwill, then the person might be lost as well, with whom we are communicating. Now if you evaluate, then you will observe, that over trying to prove a point has given us substantial losses. Also, there is a learning, from this, that, before doing anything, if we evaluate, what can we lose, then we will always refrain self from doing such things.

Friends, debates are never won by anyone in life. If you are representing yourself on a stage or a podium, and, contesting then it is a different thing. Else, we just argue from the point of view that we carry through our observation and experience. People, who are good at arguing, will always do it with flair and there is nothing wrong with that. If you are on the other side of the argument, then it is up to you, how you handle it. Are you looking to put your points forth or simply ignore them? depends. Ignoring is at times easier than to answer. This ignoring is not moving out of the conversation but handling it while not replying. On the other side, if you choose to put your points, then rest assured that you will not be listening to the entire conversation, but rather, you will start to conclude, from where you have something to prove. This is a very common human tendency.

Now let us take the second case. If you listen and ignore, and do not reply, things will always be open. By open, I mean, if things go wrong, in any discussion and you give it a patient hearing, you shall always have a second chance to amend it. Remember, those who can listen are strong people. So always develop the power to listen more. There are very few people in this world, who listen, rest all of us surely focus on expressing. A good listener is always a better decision-maker.

The Concept Of C.T.D.

I always do a C.T.D. This C.T.D. helps me to generalize life in a far better way. By C.T.D. I mean... CONNECTING THE DOTS. This is a concept, that will always help you to see things from the beginning to the end.

Just going back to my last paragraph, I have mentioned that if you listen, you shall always decide better. When you decide better, you put the best foot forward. Then, this decision-making will have all the right ingredients. That is, with C.T.D. you can visualize your start to finish. Now when you present your points to anyone, it will be a well-done job. So, you do not need to subjugate anybody by proving yourself. Even if someone wants to prove you wrong, it will not be easy to do so.

There are situations where you just can't get away with anything if someone compels you to prove something. Then listening will only be the right key to open this lock of points to prove. Many times, among our close associates or our colleagues or even in our families we are forced to prove ourselves. So here we should use listening skills and then C.T.D. Always avoid arguments, while proving yourself. If in case you feel that you are being forced to argue, then as soon as you realize, take yourself out of that. Give listening skills a priority over arguments. What is right, shall always be right. We can't change much of it, even if we try to do so.

You must add people to your life. Proving yourself can take you away from people, whereas, listening to people will help you to make you more people friendly. Also, we are not here to correct everyone, other than ourselves. It is much easy and has possibilities. Therefore, better is to work on self, than to prove and rectify others.

Remember: Let us become better humans every time, every day, every moment.

CHAPTER-16
EXCUSES.... THE BIGGEST TROUBLE

Somewhere I came across this..... *"Since EXCUSES were invented or discovered, no one is ever on the wrong side"*.

See, the moment you read this line, a smile landed on your face. This is very common with all of us. If we do not want to do anything, we have hundreds of reasons not to do it. We all have some or the other way to put the excuse. The important bit is, why do we need to do it, even when we know that, there is something wrong with, giving excuses?

The Reason For Excuses

One of the reasons for putting excuses is always the trust factor. Let us take it with an example to understand it better. In any corporate scenario, when a subordinate gives excuses for taking leave or delaying work and he misses those important deadlines, happens due to two main reasons.

The first one, is when the person is not efficient enough in understanding the work, that has been assigned to him. Sometimes, due to certain pressures in life, we tend to pick up those sections of work, in which we are not confident or even sometimes not capable enough. We presume that, while doing the work, we would start learning the same. At times, we even succeed, but, most of the time, we falter. We falter because, of the competition from our colleagues or there can be other reasons like learning and delivering at the same time. As a result of this, confidence is lost. When we lose confidence then we pick up the habit of shirking away from responsibility. This dodging from assigned work, gets us closer to lame excuses.

The Disturbing Habit

Giving excuses is always a habit, which we pick up as kids. In the very early hour of our childhood, we start developing this habit. As we grow up, this becomes a part of us in everything we do. This is so strong that we don't even realize how far we have come while doing this. We even try and prove ourselves correct, by giving excuses.

Do understand, if we are giving excuses, somewhere we could be lying as well. Therefore, this is one learning, that if we see our children giving excuses very often, then we must correct it then and there. The best possible way to solve any problem or challenge is to face it. Once we start facing it, we shall overcome the habit of giving excuse, with time.

The Fear Factor

The other reason, that we see very often is when our leaders, or bosses or seniors force us to do so. This always happens due to fear, which the superior tries to create knowingly or unknowingly. I have a good experience to share here with you. In one of my past companies, we had come across a leader who had made one of my colleagues first give excuses, then do the wrong which had gone too far to handle.

This boss was a demanding person, therefore, very often he used to ask for results with a deadline. This deadline was often associated to performing or perishing. Many would succumb to this and therefore attrition was on the higher side. This company was about acquiring business from clients. The collaterals that were required to board the clients were advance cheques. This would suffice the security purpose. One of my colleagues, who was a good performer otherwise, was just going through a rough patch. The pressure started to gradually mounting on him. His counterparts were performing, and he, who was a performer, could not do much. With the personality of our boss in mind, he then started to give false commitments and assurances. Things were not maturing and as a result, our boss started to twist his arms more often. This was becoming evident, that things will become tough in times to come. Then, after a few days, this colleague of mine started getting the security cheques. They were fake, and by the time this was realized, this colleague had resigned and moved on.

Now, see the aftermaths. The first thing was our boss was seriously questioned as to why he didn't check or got them verified. He was under a certain inquiry. The colleague, who joined some other company, had to face some legal actions. As a result of which, his current job was also lost. The sufferers of this became, their families. So, one wrong leader, and from there to the subordinate, who had been giving and picking up the wrong, and then to their families and the company, all of them suffered.

In these situations, one must stick to the righteous. See, one wrong done, due to fear, can get you in deep waters. That is what they say, "think before you act". Always double check self, what you are doing.

We must principally understand that, whenever we are giving excuses, we start to lose our credentials. The learning stops in the right direction and takes the wrong path. When our learning drifts, the development ladder also shifts from right to wrong.

Remember: Always excuse yourself from giving excuses. That's always a better form of excuse.

CHAPTER-17
TAKE IT EASY....WITH SIMPLICITY

Take it easy and live a long and happy life.

How far do we agree, simple living is not so simple to understand? Or we may say, often searching simple is not so simple. We either mix the simples or are unable to decode them. Even somehow if we happen to decode them, then the external influences in our life don't let us be sure of taking them ahead. The main reason for this to happen is, we often doubt being simple. The exaggeration in each and everything makes us feel potential. The more we exaggerate, the more we complicate, and the more we make others and ourselves confused.

Simplicity- Through Observation

The best way to learn simplicity is to observe a child. If you see a child, he or she is clear about what to do and when to do it. If they have to eat, they will do it until their stomach is full. Once it is full, they shall not take a single morsel of food after that, unlike the grown-ups. Every time we see a child, we find he or she doesn't have much work to do. To this point of mentioning, have we seen a single child who is free ever? They are super busy every time. It is just that, they do what they think they are supposed to do. Right or wrong is just defined by the adults, who observe them. A child's mind is much sorted and clear.

I have observed many people, in corporate, while they give their presentations. While giving any presentation, you can make out what life the person leads. It is the meeting room, which makes it clear about the person and the possibility of his /her growth. If the presentation has too many options or ideas, then, its complicated. So good presenters are just to the mark. They know, what to do and when to do.

The Reasons

If you see, in, and around you, you will find many people busy. They are busy and busy at times for nothing or busy due to their habit of procrastination. This is the majority. If they are busy they will want their team and people also to behave likewise. We must know what to do when to do. Once this mindset is fixed, then we must try and get that done as per the time agreed. Yes, if there is some external influence, which we can't control, then we may change the time. So, once you fix the work and then do it, you will find more time for yourself. Once you find more time, you shall be able to do more things.

A Good Example

This doing more as per your choice can only happen when you make things simple. Make them look easy on themselves and others. I have known a person, who manages his day pretty nicely. He wakes up at around 5 in the morning. Goes for exercise, and comes home, around 6:30 am. Gets his children ready for school. He is the first one to reach his office around 9:30 am. Plans his day properly. Works with his team. Manages two or three multiple businesses. Once he is back home, ensures to sit for a while with his old parents, then some looking and sorting of homework with his kiddos. Alternately, plays chess at least twice a week with his kids. Every weekend, he ensures, to play a sport for himself in the morning, then some plans with family, and also takes out time to play TT, swim or cycle as and when they call for. Every day, this person ensures to do a prayer in the morning as well as in the evening. He ensures to read at least for 15 minutes a day. He ensures to cook for his family at least twice a month.

Huh...I was amazed to know this. I asked him how he does so much. He said it is very simple, just do what you love to do for yourself. Just take it easy. If you are not able to do all, at least do some of them, what you love. He says do not see what and how others are doing. If you observe, the most common thing in his doable list is sorted, its disciplined, it's timebound. Procrastinations is to be avoided.

One must take life easy. Make it super simple, and then only can live a better living. The simplicity gets disturb when we see what others are doing. The more we dwell in others, the less shall we look at self, and more complicated we shall become. This, takes away the simplicity away from us and complicates our own self.

Few things what one must do to keep life simple is:

1. Make a simple routine, which one can follow.
2. Do not take too many tasks, which one cannot deliver.
3. Understand one's strength, and work as per the core strength.
4. Understand oneself, then one will be able to understand their people.
5. Do not bother too much on weakness, else, one will not be able to focus on one's strength.
6. Do not get confused, what others have to do or are doing, let them do. Everyone has their own way of working and have different priority towards life. One must do what one is supposed to do.
7. Pursue hobbies, at least begin with one.
8. Do not spend too much time on gadgets.
9. Spend time with family and friends.
10. Avoid disputes, learn to forgive very quickly. Forgiving is a healing process for self.

Every time, I get disturbed, I go back to my basics. By basics I mean, how and when did I start from. This can be yesterday, 5 years, 10 years or even the chirpy childhood. Past is our biggest teacher, they always guide us, make us feel strong, happy, emotional and what not. These are just so easy things, to recall.

Remember: Life is simple and easy, provided we do not make it unnecessarily super busy.

CHAPTER-18
KNOW YOUR PURPOSE

At times, it takes a lifetime to understand the word PURPOSE. Then also only a few of us can comprehend. Yes, of course, there is always a different purpose of using the word PURPOSE. I shall make my purpose very clear in what context, I am using this. My sole aim is to make one understand the meaning of what the purpose of one's life is. *What one is meant to do and what he or she ends up doing the entire life? Where do you truly find your purpose in life? How to reach there?*

Now, all these questions if coming to any human mind, shall make one confused and things will go complicated. Whenever the mind gets complicated, then the first thing that happens is, it impacts the decision-making. If your decision-making is impacted, then reaching your purpose in life depends on the decision that you have taken.

What Am I Meant To Do?

The best thing is to take one question at a time to sort the things. The first thing that one must think about is, what am I meant to do? So simple it becomes. One is meant to do that, which he or she is good at. One should be focusing on one's strengths. If anyone wants to understand the true potential of their own self, then the growing up years are the best teachers as well as the reflectors. They will always give the right picture for one's self, in which field he or she excelled. There will be times when each one of us gets drifted from the purpose of life, then again as we grow, life keeps giving us messages, to look back and realize. Many of us do come back to the purpose, and it is never easy to do so. This happens every time, be it when we understand the purpose during our childhood or later down the life. The obstacles need to be won over every time. That's how life is meant to be.

Pebbles along the Path

With purpose, comes obstacles. This is also because, when you want to achieve something in your life you might be clear on the goal, but the path which seems known, has its set of challenges when you walk down the lane. One of the biggest obstacles is called distraction. Which we need to overcome. These distractions, come to us in any form. Sometimes, it would look very dearly and sometimes they are very ugly. Ugly ones are easy to make out as we understand what ugly is. The problem comes when the distractions are dearly.

Small observation, whenever you shall plan to do something big in life, someone from your family might become a hindrance. Which is hard to understand. This might not be very intentional, but they come to you in any form. I have personally faced this many times. Whenever I have taken goals in life, there have been some known people, who stood up as obstacles in one or the other form. It is not that, I have perceived this from the universe, but, these hurdles, are the natural blocks that come on the way.

The Purpose Is Everything

They can be mental as well as physical hindrances. Then they must be confronted, and that's the only way you can get over it. The question, comes how to do so? The only thing I do is, make my purpose very strong, which the Almighty wants me to achieve. That's how I believe it. Of course, the purpose should have a good cause associated to it. You see, when your purpose to achieve anything is steady, no hurdle can be bigger than your purpose. As they say in test cricket.....Just stay at the crease, runs shall come. Do not throw away your wicket, just do not quit.

What if, when our purpose is bleak? We start fulfilling purpose of other people. That is what most of us do. There is nothing wrong with doing so. The problem arises when we do things for others and at the same time blame ourselves while doing so. When we do this, neither we sincerely are productive in fulfilling others work area, nor are we able to chase our dream. The best thing in this situation is to go with the flow. Keep doing whatever task God has assigned you at that moment. Also, keep working towards your purpose and make it so strong that, it just becomes a matter of time till you achieve it. Remember, every phase in life teaches us. This is possibly the best way which, the Almighty must have decided for you at the given moment of life. Have faith in yourself and keep chasing your dreams. The path shall be carved for you by the Lord. Possibly, this experience was needed to fulfil your purpose.

Getting Over The Shortcomings

As we move on, I find that there is one vital reason why we are unable to meet the purpose in our life. This is getting over one's shortcoming. No individual in this universe is born complete. We are all born with some or the other shortcomings. In fact if you see Helen Keller, she lost her sight and her hearing ability when she was an infant. She went on to become an Author and a lecturer. Then the bulb man, Thomas Alva Edison, developed hearing problems at the age of 12. Many more of them are there, and the list is possibly endless.

Their purpose was stronger than anything else in life. Most of us, let go our purpose due to one or the other shortcomings. Remember, shortcomings are just those undone homework that shall hound you if left untouched. So, it is better to work on those shortcomings. The purpose should be bigger always. As we have shortcomings, we have strengths as well to overcome them. People, who understand this make the most of it in life. We just need to understand what I am good at and how can I align then to overcome my shortcomings. It can be just a decision, and then you shall see things start to happen. The dream which you pursue can make wonders in your life. Leave all past baggage behind. You are as good as today. What you have achieved in the past or what opportunity you missed out yesterday or a year back or a decade back, are all gone. Everything is today so do not miss this TODAY, else it will become yesterday and go away. Utilize it to its fullest.

Remember: Just find your purpose today itself and go for it. Rest will fall into place.

CHAPTER-19
ACTION VS WORDS

There would hardly be someone who would have missed this adage... *"Action speaks louder than words"*.

We might have known it, but how much we value it, is important for us to understand. When we speak, we need to think before. Which many of us must be doing rightly. Then, do we keep a check on our actions is important to understand? Do we even notice what others are observing is critical to grab? It is critical because, when we act, we are unable to measure the depth of our expressions. Our face reflects what we think. So, thinking in the right direction is what is recommended.

Then again, mind is mind, it has all the rights to travel without our permission. You must have observed when you are talking to someone and if his mind is preoccupied with something, which has been bothering him, then you shall come to, know that physically he is present in front of you, but he is thinking something else. See, how quickly we come to know, when someone is pretending to listen and still not listening. We might be a person with a thousand faces to portray, but all of them are readable.

Observe And Absorb

Every action has something to say. It depends on how far we can go, observe, and read. Whenever you are talking to someone, you must observe the person. When you observe then only you can absorb. Words can be manipulated or modified, but actions will always have the truth to tell. Suppose you have been to a meeting at any corporate. You now have a proposal to share, concerned with the business which you are doing. The first thing is you must observe the person with whom you have the meeting. His or her way of sitting, talking, eye contact etc. If the person is interested in you, then you will immediately come to know his interest area and the meeting will go your way. Now, if this person is not showing interest then his sitting or talking posture will be different. Either avoiding or he or she might keep finding flaws in your presentation. The actions will be very prominently speaking for the person. How to handle this sort of a person is altogether a different understanding.

The Right Mind

Here, we need to understand, how can we take control of our actions and accordingly place our words. The only thing that we need to do to get this correct is, we need to have the right thinking. What we think is what is reflected. Once our thinking is in the right direction then only, we shall be able to become better human beings. Right actions are the reactions of positive thinking. When we listen to some good orator who speaks very well, he or she can only do it when they have done hours of practice in thinking in the right direction. The right mind will always speak the right words. The right mind will also do the right actions.

It is important for us to get the right understanding first on how to control our actions. Similarly, we have a clear mind to understand the action of the people, with whom we connect. One of the classic and the best ways to develop the right mind is to connect to nature. That can be in any form that you believe in. Nature is the greatest teacher, and everything around us teaches us something or the other. It depends on whether we are ready to learn. Right actions will only come through the right mind set, and the right mindset will happen when we are ready to learn. We can only learn when we unlearn. We can only unlearn when we are humble and accept our shortcomings. This acceptance will happen when we are close to nature. We cant change many things in this world, but, if we try and change ourselves, we will see the world around us is changing.

Remember: Words and action will go hand in hand, only when the thinking is right.

CHAPTER-20
DO...WHAT WE ARE SUPPOSED TO DO

This afternoon, while driving to my office, I was listening to an interesting podcast. At the same time, I had been contemplating, what should be my next topic that I should pen down. As soon as my car took the middle lane in the flyover, this gentleman in the podcast said....DO, WHAT YOU ARE SUPPOSED TO DO...and then he continued....his further talk.... and for me....it was just, like wow ! what a line...that has so much in it. We all know this but how often do we follow this?

There are mainly three questions in context to this line, that many of us would have. **Firstly,** how do we know what we are supposed to do? **Secondly,** even if we come to know what we are supposed to do, then how do we remember this every day? **Thirdly,** how to confront the obstacles that come in between this thought and us?

What We Are Suppose To Do?

I have a personal message to share here in this context. The day I decided to write this book, I was not sure if I will be able to do this or not, but, something from within kept me bothering every time to share every good thing that I have learned or have known. The you tube videos I had been making, needed to be shared in a text form. Then in the form of a book, "Gosh! I am not a writer...

I do not have the courage even to do so. How can I be in that league of writers? "All these questions and apprehensions became hurdles, which I could not think of jumping over. "This is okay, if you can't write a book, but then how could you make videos, you were neither ready for that even. Still, you managed to do it." Came the thought in the form of inspiration to me. Again, what league am I thinking about? Why do we need to be in any league or association to write something? Why am I giving so much importance to myself, even though I have not started yet?

Come on dear...no one is even judging you. Keep it very simple, You will have to do it, because you are supposed to do it. To make it more concrete within me...it stated.... "You are meant to do it. So just keep doing it, till its done." This is how it all began. What you are supposed to do is what you are best at. Your learning, your skillset, your capabilities, all these you would know the best. The only thing is, we have different learning, a variety of skills, and numerous capabilities, due to which, we get confused about what to do.

This is just so common with each one of us. We shall discuss this in how to confront obstacles. But, what you are supposed to do is what your inner self will keep knocking again and again, till you do it. The message is simple from the Universe, you will do what you are meant to do...What you seek also seeks you. So seek wisely. To do anything where you give back to society is what the universe wants us to do. Therefore, we must have a connection with nature. By Nature, I mean the Almighty. If we stay connected to Him, he shall guide us.

Yes, the most important fact is, we need to be selfless. The work is to be done, and no rewards are expected. The book has to be written, whoever reads it, depends on His wish. I can't pen even a single word without His will. He chose to write this book, it is His wish, and I am supposed to do my duty. I must be thankful and keep doing it. So, what one needs to do is a simple message from within, which is selfless and giving back every time. Each one of us are capable . It is just when are we starting it. God has given all of us some shortcomings along with certain abilities. It is between them, that we have to find, what is to be done.

How Do We Recall it Every day?

This is simple, yet complicated. Whenever we fail, in anything that we do, we must always go back to the basics. That means, from where it all started. This is the simple part that we all know. The complicated part is going back to the basics every time. Believe me, there is no other way either. Truly, the more often you go back to basics for whatever you do, the more sharper you become and the more close you come to your dutiful approach. If you do not do so, remember, that nature will keep sending messages in every way possible, till you finish it. And, it is indeed very interesting and definitely a journey worth completing. It took me a good time to complete this book, but, I had no choice left until I completed it. Going back to basics was the only way, to open the closed mind every time. Initially, I refrained as the process seemed tiring and monotonous, but I was left with Hobson's choice...and that was.....GOING BACK TO BASICS.

How To Confront?

This is the most critical part, which decides our success and failure. As I have mentioned above, we have different learning, a variety of skills, and numerous capabilities, due to which, we get confused about what is to be done, or, what work is best suited for us . If you ask me, the best way to confront is by going back to the basics every time. The moment you go back to the basics for what you know you are supposed to do is the first and only process where you challenge the obstacles. The more you reach your starting point every time, the more you are coming close to finishing the job and every time reaching the finishing line is with a vigour.

The other point is when we are not clear on what we are supposed to do. Most of us possibly keep doing something, which does not give us satisfaction. We keep working for someone, throughout life, whereas when we were meant to do something else. Though, there is nothing wrong in working for someone else, if you enjoy doing so.

The switch over, from someone's work, towards, the dream work of yours seems risky, as many of our things are at stake. The punt has to be taken and is worth it. I feel the biggest risk is not to take any risk. If we keep working for something or someone, where we are not contended, we will end up losing that work someday or the other. Then, there will be no alternative.

Now, the important part is clarity, what should be done. So, the answer is simple. There is this one thing, that will not let you sleep, which will cross paths again and again in some or the other ways, which shall be the inner voice, telling you every time, ... "*What are you doing?? I am the work that is supposed to be done. I am the work, that you are best at. I am the work, that will help you to give something to society, so please get me done.*" This inner voice is the ultimate message and we all receive it, provided we are close to the nature. When we believe in the Lord, then He takes the driver's seat and guides us.

Remember: Doing what you are meant to, shall always keep knocking till it is done.

CHAPTER-21
GOOD THINGS VS RIGHT THINGS

Good things vs Right things....how close and yet so far. If we simply ask, is everything good, right? Or if we change it a bit and then ask....can everything right, be good?? Whatever, is right will always be right. It really won't matter, if right is good or not.

Now, for instance, change in climatic conditions is a natural process and is right as well. People who are homeless, how far this change is good for them. This is something to ponder upon. In another instance, speaking the truth is the right thing, but at the same time, a lie that can save any life for better, is bigger than many truths. So, if moral values are to be considered, then both situations holds themselves right at their own stations, but what is good, is very subjective in both cases.

Actually, Good is often very idiosyncratic. This may vary from person to person, or place to place, or situation to situation. While Right is neutral, and is based on moral and ethical values. Also, any Good thing can have positive intentions, but the Right things will not only have intentions but also consequences that will be ethical. What is good in the short term, may not be the right things in the long run. Right things will always have a foresight towards the future. Anything we do right, often involves duty, which has a moral value. Good will always be a choice, which will be based on personal aspirations. Most importantly, Right things will be perpetual in various situations, but, good things, can vary from situation to situation.

Come, lets take some everyday situations to understand both of them better.

1. Getting up in the morning is a good thing, but one can only do that if they sleep in time, so sleeping in time is the right thing, from the health perspective.
2. Exercising regularly is a good thing, but doing it as per the potential strength of the body is the right thing. As each and every, body is different, so should be the exercise regime.
3. Reading a book is a good thing, but implementing the reading habit is the right thing.
4. Being ambitious is a good thing, but having the patience to fulfil one's ambition is the right thing.

Remember: Good might always not complement the right, but right thing will always complement the good. So, lets do all the right things together. Then, surely the things will be good for all of us.

CHAPTER-22
ATTRACTING THE RIGHT THINGS IN LIFE

We may agree or not, but the right thing will always be right. The right may look at times very unaffordable to many individuals, but, the essence of the rightness shall never fade. The point is, how far can we attract the right things? Or how far can we go and achieve the right things? We know what we attract, becomes a part of us.

The Basic Understanding

When we attract any specific sport in life, we will shift our focus toward the relevant sportsperson or we may search for something related to the sport on YouTube or other social media or may be in any print media. We may also find certain associations, that holds information on the sport which we are looking for.

Similarly, on the other side, if someone takes up gambling, then suddenly, he will see, that he is connecting to people, who are in that association. The challenge is not about getting attracted. The challenge lies on quitting this habit and when to stop, which is never easy. The moment we try to take a call for anything that is not right towards ourselves or society, we will observe that the association comes back to us in some or the other form. By this word association, I mean the connections that we develop, and as they say...." Old habits die hard", take a true stand and do not allow us to leave, even if we want to leave.

Meeting In Minds

This is certain that we are humans and life will always throw the possibility of choosing people. The world is full of everything, and the mix of right and not right is a blend of absolute balance. We at times, connect to a group of people, who might seem right at any point in life. Then again, as we move ahead in life, we start finding that there is a disconnect in the process of thinking. We also, realize that the energy wavelength is also not matching. This is an alarm to part ways. It does not mean that the other person or group of people are wrong, it's just, that we do not meet in minds on the road ahead. Whenever we realize this, we should move away from them. It will never be an easy call, remember. Then, the call from within should not be missed either.

People Around You

Also, we are known by the company we keep. We grow, only as much as the company grows, we will evolve, only when people around us will evolve or allow us to evolve. Therefore, in life, whenever we think, we need to move ahead, then, we must see, or should be able to see, where are we standing. Are the friends or people around us supporting you, or are they against you? Then, it becomes very clear, what to do. By moving ahead, I mean, we need to be amongst right group of people, who are better than us. This right group of people can be found through various avenues. These can be books written by great authors, some bunch of successful people, some great success stories. They would basically become an inspirational source into the journey that we take ahead.

Remember: Important is right decisions, which will be through right thoughts, then we shall attract right people. So, to attract the right....we must think right.

CHAPTER-23
CHECK YOUR RUSH

"If you are always in a hurry, life will lead you to the land of worry".

Nature is never in a rush, still, it accomplishes everything. We all possibly know that rushing for something is one of the least things in the list, which anyone would prefer. Still, in the run for livelihood, we adapt to this unwanted behaviour within us. It is more of a mob mentality, rather than an individual approach. We get influenced by looking at people who are in this format of life. They seem quite successful to the world, and whoever is successful, always influences.

Being In Rush Or Being Busy

There is a major difference between being busy and being in a rush. To be busy, we need not be in a rush, but when we rush hard, we will become busy, to match up with the rush. This pattern leads to a lot of unproductive results. Especially among the urban people, where we see everyone is in a hurry. Possibly too much to deliver in a very short time frame. Even children here are developing this habit. Which will lead to a lot of dissatisfaction and health problems. Whereas on the contrary, in the villages or small towns, people are at ease. They have the same time, and they accomplish their share of work in the day. Rural people know how to sort things better. They are contended and productive in the work they do.

Rush definitely leads to a wrong mental balance. Anger issues, strained relationships, erratic behaviour, bad health, are to mention a few from the big list of output that comes from this approach.

Simple are the ways to get rid of it. Yes, it will never happen in one day. One must keep doing the mentioned things that can change this habit. Few things which are mentioned below, actually can help.

1. Sorting out the work, what is to be done and what is not to be done. What is not to be done, is important to know. Most of us, spend time in getting this section solved.
2. What can I do, and by when can this be done. (closure timeline is very important to get the work done)
3. Make a simple routine in life, which you can follow. It need not be influenced by others. Do what you can do.
4. Understand your aspirations, many times, it gets mixed with greed.
5. Know your capability and take up the work accordingly.
6. Learn to take a break and utilize it fully.

7. Develop a hobby, close to your heart, and give it time as per your routine.
8. Listen to music, do a bit of reading at least 15 mins in a day.
9. Do your prayers daily. This removes the recklessness from us.
10. Let us recall the points from 1 to 9.

Remember: Keeping self always in rush, will eventually make one tired someday. So slow down to enjoy the rhythm of life.

CHAPTER-24
ASPIRATION VS GREED

Aspiration, if we simply understand, can be understood as ambition. Now, ambition or aspiration can be anything for any individual. It cannot be restricted in any form. One can aspire for anything. One can sets any goal in life. There are no boundaries that can be mapped. It can actually be limitless. The important thing is what one aspires to achieve. The point is what one desires. This will define the path, and the path to achieve will depend on which path one selects.

To be ambitious is always a good thing. Then the path one chooses defines the outcome. We sometimes mix aspiration with greed. And what is greed??? Greed is a desire, which is selfish and intense. It is a want for more, even what you have in abundance. This greed, when it becomes a desire, and then we aspire to fulfil it, there one takes the path, that leads to the outcome, where it is always dissatisfying. We make simple attempts to understand this, let us have a comparative approach.

Understanding Aspiration And Greed- in the form of a TREE

1. Aspiration will always have branches which will have positive ideologies, personal growth and societal betterment, without harming anyone.

Greed on the other hand will have branches, of selfish desires, ideologies which never shall matter, right or wrong, and consideration will be to better self and no giving back.

2. Aspiration will always have fruits of gratitude, a sense of fulfilment and satisfaction. Fruits of greed will be wolfish, and dissatisfying.
3. Leaves of Aspiration will breathe ethical principles. Greedy leaves will always give out, unethical and deceptive outcomes.
4. How would the flowers be? Aspiration will always blossom the happiness within. Greedy flowers will lead to temporary pleasures, whose fragrance will get eradicated in no time. The nectar of aspiration will involve responsibility and peace once achieved. Greed will not.
5. The seed of aspiration will help others to follow. It will help others to replicate and build a newer self, which will be motivating. The seed of greed, is always temporary and shall rotten up, if it cannot produce good out of what has been created.

Remember: Always aspire to create something which gives back what it takes.

CHAPTER-25
OPINION MATTERS

The only thing that comes free of cost to us is, someone's point of view. This is how we look at things when anybody shares their point of view. As we consider it to be free and that is how we perceive its value. We can say someone's point of view is somebody's opinion. This is more or less the same thing.

Every Message Counts

In any communication, there is a giver and a receiver. The giver may give anything as per his or her point of view. It always depends upon the receiver, and how one takes it. This is very simple for us to understand. Every opinion is bagged by some or the other information that has been collected from some source. This source can be genuine at least to an extent, the rest of the sharing, can be cooked or created.

A fine receiver must know how to filter the points. To filter, the receiver has to be a good listener. They say....and I too follow....*LISTENING IS A FINE ART*. Once we listen, we can keep the relevant things and leave the things that are not required. There have been times, when we all must have had a situation, where, we have said to ourselves..." Thank God, I heard this message.

Had I missed it, it would have been a real problem for me".

So every message counts. Every message is important. We know all good things come in small packets. The universe tries every time to share the message, what can be good for us. We must know how to filter it and take the right out of it. What are the benefits of someone's opinion?

- The first thing when we listen, we avoid arguments.
- The listener is always a great friend. The opinion-giver will love it.
- When we listen to any opinion, we can figure out, what can be good for us. There could be points, which the receiver, might have even not thought of.
- The more opinions given, the better it becomes for us to select. As the choices are more so are the possibility of doing right. However, some of us would think that too many choices will make our decision-making poor. Then again, the filter concept to select the less out of many is an excellent tool.
- When we listen to the opinion that is given, helps us to understand the person better. We know, what is one thinking, how is one thinking, is the person right enough to bond with. We can

plan a better approach against that person to handle him or her. Many superiors or friends or family members, can be evaluated as a person when we listen to their point of view. We then know, the right way to tackle them.

Remember : Opinions are like rivers, that flows from any direction. It is for the wise to understand, filter and use it for wisdom.

CHAPTER-26
LESS IS MORE

Yes, at the first go, there is a disagreement- How can less be more? We always aspire for more. More of everything. More of money, more of spending, more of happiness, more of knowledge, more of life, more of inspiration, more of motivation. So everything more. Then how can this be so convincing?

Simple And Complex Things

This is true that life is all about aspiration, but how much is to aspire for, should be known. How much can we rightly manage, should be clear to us. The more we desire for, the more things become complex. We are often not ready to manage the complexities of life. We aim, we grow, we get complexed, and then we refute. The more we aim for, the less we stay simple and the more we get complicated. Things are meant to be as they are. We need to wait for the right time to do the right things. In my next chapter, this will be much clearer and specific to you as a reader.

I quote an example here. Suppose someone is very hungry, and all of a sudden a very delicious dish, which this person likes is served in front of him. Now this person starts to gobble up. In minutes he finishes the served plate. Now, if you ask him how he is feeling after having the meal. The person will take no time and say, I was so hungry, now I am feeling good. Thank God the hunger is gone. If you observe, at the first go it's hunger that is prioritized more than the taste. When the food was being eaten, the person could hardly feel the taste.

Now we turn the tables and change the situation. The food served is in small quantity, and the person is still hungry. He would still consume, as the hunger is there, but, the thought would be different. This time when you ask yes what is it that you want? The person would say I would want some more, its really very delicious and I am still hungry, considering the chef has done a good work while preparing. When we have few things we truly cherish it's important, anything in abundance is hard to manage and can lead to wastage.

When Things Are Adequate

We must see all things that we are capable of doing, rather than taking more and delivering less. When we have adequate in our hands and do justice to the available things, we will be far more successful and things will be much rewarding. By less, here I mean, adequate, which is sufficient for anything to relish. This adequate is easy to handle. When something is easy to handle, it produces better and greater results. Things have to be much simpler. The more simple the things are, the less stressed one would feel. Growth is a must and there is no denial on that. Then we must know, which way to walk to get that growth.

Aspire for more, but what to aspire for, must be very clear. Trust your own self, understand your capabilities, know your strength. Once you do these, you grow and manage better. Sorting is essential.

Remember :When you can handle less, then less will give you more. This less, which is more is never-ending and truly inspiring.

CHAPTER-27
LAST EVENING, YESTERDAY ENDED

Some of us or let me put it this way, most of us love to boast on our past. If we have achieved something down the lane in our life, gives us a great joy and satisfaction. Life is full of ups and downs, and we always have some things to admire as well as repent for. Our entire life depends on what we have achieved or even missed out on. Things achieved, certainly give us a sense of satisfaction. Every success counts. Every time we remember our success, we feel proud. Moreover, if we share it, it feels even better. Especially when we share it with people who look up to us.

On the contrary, how many of us love to talk about our past failures? Do we even want to remember how many times we had failed? This chapter of failure, only opens when we become successful in life, else, it is better not to open up, that is what we believe in. None of us want to fail. We all want to be successful. Important is, that we all want to be successful in everything we do. We carry all success, from our past, and that is what we want to replicate. This replication is done with the thought process from past achievements. The question comes, how do we deal with a new circumstance? How do we succeed then? What application should we take from the past to get it resolved?

It Was All Yesterday

Yes, it is important to understand that yesterday ended last night. Everything that we have gained or lost is over for every new day. This is very clear to the sportsperson. They know the way to switch over from their past. They treat every day as a new one. They carry the experience from the past but not any recognition. They know every challenge is different, every game and every day will be different. We must know one thing, what has taken us here won't take you there. This "there" is the next step or dream that people want to fulfil.

Victories & Failures

If every victory counts so shall be every failure. In fact, if we can accept failures its even better. The cricket great of all times, Sachin Tendulkar, must have practiced that cricket-shot or stance many times, in which he got out. That made him so different and the best-ever batsman, with the century of centuries he has in his kitty. Its all about that simple practice that makes us stand out. The more we accept it, the stronger the foundation becomes. I remember and repeat those classic lines from Brucelee- " *I do not fear the man who has practiced 10,000 kicks once, but I fear the man who has practiced one kick 10,000 times*". The best way to move forward, is to realize the faults from the past and correct us for future for more concrete outcome.

Achieve Give And Achieve

Yesterday, if we had some great day, it should be an experience to share, not a possession. It should help others to learn, rather than claiming it for oneself. Remember, the more we keep it to ourselves, the lesser we move ahead. The more we let go the achievements in our mind, then there is always something again to achieve. If one has got awards for something great done, it should be done and dusted. One has to perform to give it back . The more we give, the better we become. Failures must bother us from our past. That means the task which is incomplete and must be done. The message from the universe is clear, it will keep sending you information through its medium, to complete the task. You need to pass the bridge where one side was a baggage of failure and the other side you will see success. Remember, success is always about the journey not the destination reached. Achieve it, and give away, to achieve again, and give away and go on doing this. One who does that brings change to the world.

Remember: Today is a new day, a new opportunity, a new fight. If you want to perform today, then fight it with your experience, not with the mind or head where there is success. Experience is permanent, success or failure is always temporary. It's all about getting the work done which is yet to be completed.

CHAPTER-28
EVERY CRISIS IS AN OPPORTUNITY

They say *"Amid every problem or challenge, lies the solution"*. If there is a need then it becomes a driving force for new inventions. Had there been no darkness, the bulb would not have been created. This is perhaps one of the finest examples, that I have come across. Crisis is always need-based. In other words, we can say if there is a need that is marked, then it will be just a matter of time, the inventions or the solutions will come. The only thing which is important here, if the need is mine, are we the ones, who can take and understand the opportunity to invent? This approach shall make us different. It is here, that most of us are stuck or are not able to visualise.

Understanding Crisis

Any crisis is natural and inevitable and so are opportunities. I believe, that if a crisis has occurred, that means, something good is round the corner and is just about to happen. Yes, change is certain. We also term crises as problems. The more power we give to adversities or problems, the more the solutions go away from us. I have stated it earlier as well, we must learn to say a problem as a challenge. Then the contest between us is fifty-fifty. It will be a fight worth it. Otherwise, when we say challenge as problems, then problems will always be on the upside of the hill and position itself as advantageous.

What Does Crisis Do?

Any crisis has its character traits. The moment it arises, it makes us uncomfortable. For example, when we face the extreme heat during summers, we generate a need for an air conditioner, and in winter we prefer the other way round. It will be a heater or a blower requirement to beat the cold. A crisis makes one nervous and we start panicking . This is very common in extreme situations. We must not give up and hang on.

We must accept the crisis. Most of the time, we are hesitant to accept and acknowledge. We simply quote it as a problem and move away from the solution. We restrict ourselves from the solutions. The best way to understand and combat crises are the following:

Skill Set

All of us are gifted with some or the other skill sets. We accept it or not, our skills are our best weapons and we must trust, understand, and know how to use them. If we look for any opportunity during the crisis, we can always do it with the skills that we have. For example, suppose, someone loses a job and he is a great guitarist. So one can find this as a second source of income by teaching or playing guitar. Certainly, it might not match the level of the income last drawn, but, then its an opportunity during the crisis that has happened, and who knows, it take you miles in your success journey.

Preparation Is Always The Key

Forewarned is forearmed. We must always be prepared for the worst. The worst is uncertain and can be lethal. It can't be predicted either. Still, keeping oneself prepared for anything is always good. Possibly, at times we might not foresee the situations, but, then unnerving would make it worse. So, We must calculate at least the known shortcomings that we have. For example, someone who plans to do business must know, what could be the possible challenges that one should address. If we can plan at least 50% of them, we are always at a better position to address them.

Strong mindset

The most important factor is to have the right mind frame. People, who do not give up make the difference. They always have a different lookout towards life. They take up challenges. They will always seek opportunity and try to create something out of every challenge. It's a never-giving-up attitude that marks the difference.

Remember: Winners do not do different things, rather they do the same things differently. Every Crisis has an opportunity, just keep looking till you find it.

CHAPTER-29
DEADLINE MATTERS

There is nothing like a deadline, which keeps one going. It is one of the great motivating factors, to attain anything that we aspire for. Deadline requires commitment and every commitment needs courage to fulfil. Most of the time, we shirk away from committing. As soon as we commit, it will require work and work is something that has to be done. This is where the winners differentiate themselves from the rest. Winners commit and commit within a time frame. When a time frame is blocked, then only the planning will happen. Once planned, then executions takes place. This is very important for each one of us to learn. What happens when a deadline works as a motivator?

Sense of Responsibility

As we have a deadline, it gives a sense of responsibility. The moment we take ownership, things start to fall into place. Responsibility has its own power. When it amalgamates with the power of deadline, wonders happen. In fact, this combination is so powerful that it takes on any challenge that comes in the path of success. There is a never giving up attitude, till the task is complete. Responsibility will only come when there is a sense of ownership. This makes the difference.

Sense of Urgency

With ownership, comes the sense of urgency. It gives one a push to finish within time. The reputation matters here. Once committed then there is no looking back. Also, the person here knows what to do when. The driving plan and executing plan complements each other. If either of the one is missed, then the other upcoming part will suffer. This sense of urgency keeps one on toes till the work gets completed.

Mapping Progress & Productivity

The moment, we have ownership and urgency, we grow a step ahead. The result of any work will only come when we have a deadline to make up for it. The result is the last in the tick box for which we are working. But the productivity will start to show, as soon as we take the ownership to complete the deadline. How far have we come, and how much to go, can be gauged through productivity only. Mapping one's progress, helps one to take the right required steps and alter things, if it is needed.

Sense of Satisfaction

As we see the progress, the feel-good factor comes into play. This further gives a push to complete the task within the deadline. It is here at this stage, we start to think beyond the deadline. As if it is already achieved. Now, what after the work is done? One can see beyond the achievement now. This is where a sense of satisfaction comes, where we acknowledge to ourselves, yes this is the right path.

Sense of Encouragement: Whenever we have achieved anything in due time, it has always stood as an inspiration. This inspiration works as a great motivator for future endeavours. Here we know, what to do and how to do or how to complete things as per the deadline. Therefore, to achieve anything in life, deadline matters, else the essence of success is lost, if not done within time. Always have a backward integration approach. As you take a goal, take the deadline as well and stick to it till you have achieved the sense of encouragement, the last step of the above five mentioned.

Remember: Success and work done can be simply differentiated, one which is done within time agreed is success otherwise it is a work done.

CHAPTER-30
BALANCING WORK LIFE

There is always an outline for all of us, we must have a work-life balance. This means we must give adequate time to work and also celebrate the goodness of life. Now, how composite are these two and how does their combination work?

People work either for themselves or for others. Then we break it further, as discussed in my earlier Chapter about ABC (Area Beyond Control) or AUC (Area Under Control), when we work for others, we are controlled by others, and that is ABC. When we work for ourselves, still external factors rule us. So, being self-employed is AUC, but due to extensive external intervention, it becomes ABC to an extent. If the entire process is managed by external factors, the question comes, how would we balance work & life? To balance work with life and by life I mean a great life just not a good one, we must have the right distribution of time for work and other factors of life.

Work And Life- What If....

What is work? we all know. What is life? and how we celebrate it? is what we should know. What if, when we have good amount of money ? When we have enough money and time, which we can spend at our will. We can keep enjoying long holidays and no one is there to bother. When we have a sufficient amount and we do great charities. Just by reading this, one must be feeling good, and just imagine, when we actually have it, how would it be? For this, the statement has to be different and simple. Let us rewind: Can work balance life? this is the question and the answer is .....probably when you work for yourself and you work as per your choice, you work becomes your life, and it starts to shower everything that you aspire for. When you love what you do, then the passion is very different. Then it is not work anymore, it is life that balances your work. What we should do to make work our life. Let us think that way.

There are only a few of us, who are fortunate enough, to do what they want to do always. For example, if someone wanted to play chess at an early age and had been doing it throughout life, then life is already balanced. Playing chess possibly to him is no more work, it is rather the life that he or she would aspired for. The question comes, can we do it for ourselves? If yes then how?

Follow your passion
Do what you want to do. As we grow up, we start to develop a belief, that the dream that we had when we were all children, is no more possible. I have a different perspective on this. If there is a dream, then it is already within us, and we just need to stay there till we make it. Every dream has a reason, if we just stick and keep

pursuing it, then it is just a matter of time it happens. Someone had a dream to open a company and he did it when he was 60 years old after a lot of struggle. It's late but it is still worth it. It is never too late to achieve something that we live for. Whatever are the circumstances, we must keep our passion alive.

What you seek, seeks you as well
Keep yourself redefining and reinventing. Times change and so does we. We must keep seeking as, what we seek is actually seeking us. We just need to believe ourselves, then we will notice that what we were looking for was actually looking for us as well.

Limiting Distraction

This attraction of distraction, is one of the biggest challenge. This distraction, is the biggest foe, for our dreams that can make or give a great life. What does not help us get the right life, that we aspire for has to be kept aside. We can and should only attract the right things that can make our dream happen.

Remember: If we do what we love, then the life than will come out of it, shall be a life worth living. Let us look for work that we love, life will get balanced.

CHAPTER-31
GREAT VS GOOD

Since we have known time, GOOD & GREAT have always been fair rivals. Whenever, life is ordinary, we will want it to be good but shall always aspire for great . The journey from good to great, is always aspirational, but it requires certain level of self-belief. It also requires some non-negotiable sacrifices & coming out of our comfort zones. It is important for us to understand, that if we look for a great life, the good has to be given up. We can also say that if we want a great life, it will require some extraordinary efforts. These efforts can only be given, when we decide to move out of our comfort zone. Most of us, get stuck with this word- extra ordinary. We fear or avoid this.

Then again, if we see, we all have been doing the extra bit in each and everything we do in our day-to-day life. The only difference will be, we do it unknowingly. Also, when we see the great life of people in and around us, we get inspired and fascinated. Great life is very subjective to every individual as per their aspirations. Some would look for a lavish life as a great life, and some would just want a simple life, which will be great to them. A simple understanding for both will make it clearer. If we compare them, then both have their own importance.

Come, let us see for ourselves, how their comparative study can help us to understand them.

1. **Effect or Influence** they leave upon :

Great life will always have a significance and a possibility of a higher longevity. The legacy can be transferred from one generation to another.

Good life will be positive, good and nice, then again, they are limited to the existing generation only. The next generation has to build up everything from the beginning.

2. **Quality** of life that one has :

Great life will have a cream and outstanding life as far as quality is concerned. In a great life there will always be a choice, what one wants to do? How one wants to spend the life? If someone wants to be on a vacation, then one can be there as per his or her choice of time. There is generally no bindings. The materialistic factors have a greater probability to be fulfilled here.

Good life will be satisfactory, and one shall be accepting life as per the situation. The quality of life here is also good, but an element of compromise will be there. The good part here is, one will always be aspiring for more in comparison to great life. This aspiration generally can change the existing circumstances and the probability of growth factor is very high here.

3. **Recognition** in both the cases:

Great life is generally celebrated and is always motivate others. Though they have their own set of challenges. One whose life is celebrated, is not a free bird. They cannot come out in public whenever they wish to. Most of the celebrities, have this problem. A great life has the power to guide as well as inspire others.

Good life has a proficiency and is always comfortable. There is no big burden of image to carry, which makes one much easier and the freedom is a blessing here. This is the zone for higher skills and talents. If one must go to the great life, the journey shall begin here.

4. **Effort** has a role to play:

Great life will require extreme efforts and will always ask you to be out of your comfort zone. People here are more disciplined and put more dedication in whatever field they belong to. There is just five percent people in the world who reach here. People are more challenge oriented here. The finest part of Great life is, most of the people here know, how to build up themselves and how to stay focused towards their goals. The quality of leadership and ownership is much high in this zone. They also have a higher appetite to take risk and proceed further in life.

Good life will require consistent effort. The comfort zone here is something which people cherish and find it as a protection, inside that they cocoon themselves.

People generally do not challenge the existing factors. The risk-taking hunger is much lower but, those who have the guts to take risk here, change the world and have been the real heroes in times immortal.

5. **Value** addition

Great life can always add value to others life. These are the people who can support the needy and can-do great charity to the world. In fact, there have been many great people in the history of mankind, who have contributed to life of others either through money or knowledge. Great life doesn't mean only having a lot of money. It also means to people who have great wisdom and have shared their knowledge to the world, for a better place to live in.

Good life also adds value to the people who aspire for a good life. They have limited resources therefore the contribution is also considerate. People here are more satisfied and can do their bit as per their limitations in contributing towards the world. Good life is also aspirational for the people who are needy and look up to a better life.

Remember: Life is all about giving back to the society. The choice is ours, how and in what way we want to contribute. If we understand our true self, then we all have the possibility and strength to contribute in all good faith. The more we contribute, the better shall become our journey, from ordinary to good and then to great.

CHAPTER-32
EVERYTHING HAPPENS FOR A REASON

Whatever happens, happens for good.

This faith is mostly claimed be the sanguine group of people. They have a very powerful way to take on things. There are always two ways to look at things. The first one is, when a person always finds a reason for everything happening . This can be good or bad, irrespective, and accordingly the acceptance or denial comes. The other mindset is, there must be a reason, what has happened and accepts it . So, the look out towards the reasons in both cases are very different. We can make or break our future just by exploring either of the factors.

Reason

Let us understand the word reason. It can have many synonyms like cause, motive, basis, logic etc. The more we delve into it, the more it gets complicated. If we find the "**cause**", we generally add a "because" to it as per our convenience. If we figure out the word "**basis**", then we tend to move towards arguments. for example ..." on what **basis** the company has taken this action against me", is a statement, which someone may ask in his office. And if we find "**logic**" then most of efforts goes into calculations where solutions are negligible.

Now, how about "**motive**". This certainly gives an extension of the word which changes our perspective. Motive becomes "motivation". All the other three words except motivation, move our thinking towards questioning self. When we question ourselves, we may land up into the weaker side of our personality. This makes us weak and away from believing in the possibility.

Now let us see, what benefits can we have if we start believing that...... Everything Happens For A Reason.

Promotes positive mind set: Whenever we look into any reason with a positive mindset, we become more solution oriented rather than being problem seekers. This helps us learning from the experiences and we change towards becoming better human being.

Promotes Resilience: One becomes much stronger, and the mind set to bounce back from an adverse situation becomes very strong. People come out tougher and better. This resilience and never to give up, are the steps towards growth.

Provides Opportunity: Crisis is the mother of all inventions. All the best possible solutions in the world have only come from the biggest crisis. The ordinary became the extraordinary when they saw reasons as opportunities and made the right choices to take this up as motivation.

Regret factor gets dissolved: It reduces the regretting factor as people take ownerships for every outcome. They make this as an essential approach for their growth. They see it as a learning curve during their journey towards their goal.

Builds up the belief level : As the regret factor reduces the acceptance towards the situation is cultivated. As we accept the situation, we start believing self and start to trust the Supreme power. This further reduces our stress and anxiety and the purpose of life becomes very significant.

Remember: Accepting situations and facing it with vigour shall make one a productive human.

CHAPTER-33
PRESENT IS THE REFLECTION OF THE FUTURE

"As you spread, so shall you reap"

What we do today, shall be the outcomes of tomorrow. The present is just not a fleeting moment but an important reflection for tomorrow. Today is never transitory but has a reason always. Everything in this world happens for a reason, this I have already stated in my last chapter. It is how we put ourselves today for a better tomorrow. Life is always uncertain and so is the future. The only certitude that we have today is to act. Life is all about results and results are produced based on actions done. Each action we take today, based on decision made, will be our potential future tomorrow.

Now, let us evaluate together, what are the factors that illustrate and can shape our future.

Routine and Habit

Aristotle says- *"We are what we repeatedly do, excellence then is not an act, but a habit"*. Every successful person in this planet, must have diligent routine and sincere habits, else success will never be possible. Routine and habits, creates consistency and stabilizes us. When we fall into a routine pattern, then it sets our mind and body clock accordingly. This routine becomes a habit. It builds up efficiency and enhances productivity. Interestingly, the procrastinating mind sees a back seat, when we empower routine and habit.

Decision Making

We always have a choice in life, these choices make the person that we are. The choices that we are making today controls our future. Now, let us club the two points that we just mentioned together. Suppose, from tomorrow morning some of us decide to exercise regularly, and make it a habit, how would that be? We keep doing it consistently for six months, now how would that be? Now, imagine we make it a routine, and do it religiously every day. Imagine, yourself doing it for five years, and just feel your body doing so, how would you feel? Isn't this fantastic. Therefore, the decision taken five years ago, has given you some result, which is worth cherishing. We all know, what is right for us, and when we know that, then making a choice becomes simpler.

Actions Taken

Action is the only driving force behind every plan. Every action that we shall take today will set off our tomorrow. Actions taken will be giving outcomes. Every outcome is important. They are our best teachers. We must think of the result first and then take our actions. Now, if we see, the decision taken without any action plan leads us nowhere. Thus, action is a must. While we take actions and then culminate it with habits and routine, now the outcomes are fantastic. The growth is certain and then there is always experiential learning for self to grow and others to follow. It leaves a definite legacy for the next generation to take up. The action that is taken at the right time will make us more positive. The experience that we gain out of our learning, teaches us to handle things better.

Remember: Today the choices made will become tomorrow's reality....therefore, choose wisely.

CHAPTER-34
HUMILIATION HAS A PURPOSE

They say, *"The tallest tree catches most of the wind"*.

As we grow in life, we face many things. Everyone has an opinion, and they opine for someone who has a face in the crowd. Those who take risks, may face criticism or humiliation as well as appreciation. It is up to every individual, how they handle them. No one wants to be humiliated or criticized. In fact, any humiliation if we remember in life, in case we have come across, we refrain it to recall even.

Seek Healing

Similarly, if we have humiliated someone, how often do we remember that? This is an important retrospection and if we recall, to hurt someone, then we must apologize. This is for our own self-healing. The moment we remember of hurting someone, that means the forgiveness is still due and we are yet to start the self-healing process. Therefore, it is better to seek forgiveness and that is how we shall seek healing for self. This is what we can do at our part.

The next question, is what is to be done if someone humiliates us & in case if they are on a higher authority from us and we could do nothing but face it ?

Questioning Self

The next most important question comes, why me always? I feel, there must be a purpose behind every humiliation that we go by. Depends how we take it. In many offices the bosses humiliate their subordinates time and again, and this is for sure those who humiliate, should never expect results. If they somehow do, then they themselves would not know what the expected outcome would be. People humiliate others, out of a revenge mindset or they get pleasure hurting others.

Impact

Humiliations can serve as an impactful facilitator for growth and self-awareness. In fact they are the catalyst towards developing better resilience and humility. In some cases, humiliation acts as a wakeup call. However, it is important to distinguish between constructive experiences that brings growth or destructive moments, where criticism harms someone. In the latter case the wrong effects can far outweigh any proper benefits. Ultimately, humiliation can have a purpose in life, but the impact will depend on how one responds to it.

Now, let us figure out, how and why there is always a purpose behind of what is happening. Everything happens for a reason, so possibly humiliations is one of the reasons.

Humiliation nurtures humility and humbleness. this is one of the finest human behaviours, which becomes a reason for personal growth.

Humiliation builds resilience and increases tolerance. Humans have some great habits.... like, what we learn here, we use there. So with criticism, comes the power to overcome the emotional pain, which makes us strong for our future challenges.

Humiliation helps us develop empathy for others. One who goes through this phase, knows how it would feel on others. With empathy, we make the world a better place to live.

Humiliation makes one more capable to respond to similar situation in future rather than reacting towards the situation.

It was the humiliation only what Tulsidas suffered, and nature had a purpose behind. Tulsidas went on to pen down Ramcharita Manas, which is an epic poem. Humiliation is certainly the least thing, that anyone would want. This comes to anyone, when one is not much prepared to face it. Then it has to be handled. Someone, who is wrong or created a crime, and this person is getting humiliated, this all is a different context. Doing wrong and getting humiliated, is more of a deserving of punishment, and it is not humiliation. Then if someone gets framed wrongly, and is facing humiliation, is a point of concern. This cannot be avoided, so this has be dealt with.

Remember: Humiliation is a powerful weapon to reinvent self, adopt the right values, chose the right path, and strengthen the character.

CHAPTER-35
DISCUSSION FOR ARGUMENT OR SOLUTION- CHOICE IS OURS

Discussion if done fruitfully, it will become a centre of prudence.

The purpose of discussion, generally varies, depending upon the perspective. Ideally, every discussion is done with a purpose. It is done to reach a consensus or try and find the solution. It will always be a collaborative approach and must have two or more people to get it done.

However, discussions sometimes devolve into arguments. This happens when the participants focus more on winning or try to prove a certain point. When this happens, discussions become more of defending self-position rather than getting into the common ground. Then we can call discussions a form of debate or dispute or disagreement.

Discussions generally should help us get the solutions and people who want solutions will always try and come to the common ground. We must understand first, why do we get into discussion? Of course it would be to find out a solution. Then again, most of us land into arguments and why this happens? We must understand, if we are looking for solutions then we will have to listen more and speak less. Now, we often tend to do the opposite and lose out on getting many good points, which could have been a solution for us. We somewhere have a belief within that, those who speak are valued as intelligent people. Therefore, we often take up the opportunity to speak more than to listen. Remember, listening is always a fine art.

Now, let us see how discussion is helpful when we listen.

The first thing that happens is, we do not give an opportunity to argue. If anyone even deliberately tries to do so, will not succeed. Anyways, as they say....*mutes do not have enemies.*

Then, secondly, it promotes understanding of people better which helps us to collaborate with likeminded people. We become better in judging people.

Thirdly, a good listener is always a good leader, or we can say a good leader must always be a good listener. This will help to take a righteous decision out of any discussion.

Fourthly, when one listens during discussions, then there is always a high probability to gain more creative and innovative ideas. One such example comes to my mind while penning this down....it happened so, that in one of the meeting for a big toothpaste company, they were discussing on how to increase the sales considering its competitor's performance. In that discussion, one of the employees had shared a weird idea of making the mouth of the paste a bit broader and bigger, so that more paste could come out and more usage happens. Many of his colleagues might have laughed at this idea, but this was sold to the management. This is how, a weird idea became a creative and innovative idea. This could only happen because the leaders down there were solution seekers and great listeners.

Finally, in any discussion there are two outcomes positive and negative. The more we listen and avoid arguments the chance of getting towards positive side is higher.

So, these are stepwise approach on how we should understand the importance of discussion. We must also realize that discussion which is to be done, is even worth doing or not. If we do not contribute in any discussions, it's better not be a part of that discussion.

Remember: A good discussion will always light the path of understanding.

CHAPTER-36
EXPECTATIONS- CAN BE THE REASON FOR DISAPPOINTMENT

Expectations can be a root of all heartaches. We all have expectations and that is how it is meant to be as well. Without expectations, how can we expect life. In fact, life is all about expectations. When we have high expectations, which are unrealistic or misses proper communications, we often land into disappointment. This can further lead to frustration or even resentment. Antipathy is one of the main reasons which happens when expectations are not met.

The Right and The Wrong

Before having any kind of expectation, from anyone, we must understand two things. First one is, the expectations set must have an element of authenticity. Next one, the person against whom the expectation is set must be capable enough to fulfil the expectation. In both the cases, it will create a sense of loss if expectations are not met. Most of us have expectations from our children irrespective of their age. This is a legacy that has been carrying since time immemorial by humans. Now, if we consider both the above cases of reality and capability, then we will be able to figure out if the expectation is right or not.

Let me make it more clear for us to understand. When a child is born and grows up as a toddler and starts doing something which is eye catching, then we expect him or her to perform in front of other people. As the child grows, then we expect him or her to compete as per the other children in our nearby surroundings. We will try out all possible means to make them, do every activity which we ourselves might not be capable enough to do. But then, we try to bring in all possible sources and equipment for our child to be better. As they grow up and get settled, now we expect them to take the responsibility which we have carried so far. This is again to be monitored as per their capability and reality. Because as time changes, so does the circumstances. Things what our parents did, might not be done by us and what we are doing, our children might not connect to them. Therefore, we many a times unknowingly set up wrong expectations, and then the results are disappointing.

Let us figure out some points what happens when we set wrong expectations.

Handle Disappointment

This is the most common outcome of wrongly set expectation. We have major disappointments which can further lead to frustrations and even animosity. Think of any situation where you had set expectation from someone and then it was not fulfilled. Now, you might not want to remember it even. If you recall it in your memory album, then you would often like to go back and change it. Disappointment restricts us from experimenting or exploring .

Impacts Relations

When we set up wrong expectations in personal or professional fronts, it can lead to disagreements, clashes and misunderstanding with people around us. Which can go further in life without any healing and the trust which gets broken once becomes hard to mend. If we observe, then we can see many households have this problem. When a couple falls in love they have different set of expectations. As soon as they get married, the level of expectations changes. Divorces are one of the unwanted products of wrongly set expectations. This could be from either of the spouse or even the extended families of them. So, on the lighter side, now as a reader be careful, how far you should fulfil expectations and set your level against your spouse.

Anxiety and Stress

With the above two points (*Disappointment and Strained Relationship*), comes stress and anxiety. This leads to health issues further. The growth and learning also gets impacted as the courage to deliver through self, takes a back seat.

It is always better to believe in self. We must be capable enough to do the work ourselves. As a leader, which we all are, we must know how to get the work done and learn to delegate the job rightly as per capability. The more we depend on others, the more expectations we will have from others, the more we will set wrong expectations.

Remember: It is better to rely and expect from self and with self, you can always give a second chance to fulfil things.

CHAPTER-37
PAUSE- THE DIMOND RULE

Silence is Golden and most of us know this proverb. In India, precisely in the rural sectors or the country sides, children often play a game, where they say "times up.... times up" and everything stops for a moment. This temporary stop makes every child (who are playing) to restart the game. But when they stop, they would not even blink their eyes, they would stand still for a while wherever they are till the call gets over.

This moment of stop is otherwise called "PAUSE". I understood and related it much later in my life. This pause was a brilliant invention in that frame of the game. It made every player reboot themselves. The first thing that this pause did was, it created an opportunity. The opportunity for the non-performer to perform better and for the performer to retain the performance. It created a small drinking water break or a loo break as well. It also gave a chance to change some of the rules, which as a child, many would differ. "I have been the den for good number of times, now someone else should take up, and remember, this time, the area of play or the vicinity would be more", shouted one child out of the bunch. Some would agree some would not. But post the pause, things changed.

Pausing is an art and a master stroke in every field of life. Once I asked a gentleman, out of the two, ear and mouth, what do we prefer to use more? He said, "while in conversation with my wife, I have only choice to use my ear and she uses her mouth, she even speaks my share of words as well". Now, with this I am certain that all husbands would know how to save themselves.

When To Pause

Most of us have a challenge in understanding when to pause. We often pause, when we are supposed to speak. Also, at times, there are situations, where we keep speaking without taking a break. This break if taken at the right junctions can really make up for many things.

Let us understand, the benefits of pausing. I shall try and explain it from a speaker's point of view.

The Time Factor

As a speaker, in any stage or a public forum, there have been many instances where I had drifted away from the topic. This is very natural with everyone. Drifting away. Some of us realize it while others might not. Very common thing, but this changes the course of the topic. The best way to come back to focus is **pause.** Now pause must have a limit. If it exceeds more than expected time, then the flair or interest is lost in the topic. It should not be more than 3-5 secs ideally. As soon as you pause, your confidence comes up, so does the relevance. In case there has been a drift, then the speaker gets time to settle down.

Pause But Do Not Stop

This works other way round as well. If you run short of words while speaking at a forum, just **pause**. You would find the right required word to speak. This is in fact, one of the most used tactics and approaches which is used by the most sorted speakers around the world. It becomes obvious as well, that when we run short of words we stop. We need to convert our mind from accepting stop to accept pause. So now onwards, if we are speaking at any forum and we have a probability to go short of words or have a possibility to forget, then we will pause and not stop. This will keep it going till we as a speaker want to close it.

Sorting Anger

Next when we get angry, we must **pause**. The more you pause the better it will be. Here the time limit, is very different from the above. This is different because the circumstances are different. This is one of the most difficult things to do, but if adopted then this is the best things that we can do to ourselves. Pause, makes anger use as a tool. As we apply pause, we would rightly know how and when to use the anger. Anger will be more usefully utilized rather than being wrongly used.

Further, if we note, every pause gives us a better clarity of thought. We organize better in adverse and complex conversations.

Cutting Down Fillers

As a speaker , when we present ourselves in front of the audiences or people, we come short of words as I have mentioned above. Then, we unknowingly start using fillers like..."Umm or Ahhh and so on". So, using pause effectively improves our communication. This makes the speaker and the listener both comfortable.

Remember: If silence is the golden rule, then, Pausing is the diamond rule.

CHAPTER-38
F O C U S

"The man who moves mountains, begins by carrying away small stones".

This famous Chinese proverb meant- Great tasks requires persistence and focused efforts. I have heard many people saying that- I shall now onwards focus on my work. This word "F O C U S" take its birth at a very early stage in every individual's life.

The Confused Concept

As I remember, when I was a child, I was told by my teachers and parents to focus on studies. What they meant was somewhat different to me from what I understood. What I understood is very interesting for me to share. When I was a child, we often used table lamps for the purpose of study. Now, this lamp, had a bulb, which was not seen from the above of its holder and as soon as you would switch it on, it glowed beneath the holder, and used to illuminate the table from a foot ruler distance above it. Then, when you place a book below the light, it was very bright, and the entire text were easily readable due to this sufficient light. We could say the focus of light was spread all over the book, as it did not spread anywhere other than the focused area. So, if anyone told me to focus on studies, I used to feel myself as that bulb from one of the table lamps, who is spreading the light over the textbook just by staring over it. My focus of staring at the book was very bright just as the lamp, but the results/outcomes were not that bright. So, to me focus meant, to look or stare the book, or for that matter anything, in similar situations.

The Clear Example

Now, when we ask someone to focus, what do we mean is important. As a child, I remember, I was very fond of movies. During my vacations, I got a good opportunity to watch movies. My boarding school, like any other boarding schools, had some limitations, and especially in the primary wing. We rarely had a chance to see new movies. When my vacations got over, and as I went back to my school, all my friends would gather around me, and I would narrate them the story of the movie, which I had seen during holidays. It used to be very dramatic and interesting for my friends to listen to the plot. I would act, give the relevant dialogues, make myself emotional as per the scenes. Not even a single screen would be missed during my narration. It was an apt story telling. The results/ outcomes were very satisfying to me and my friends.

It took me a while to understand this word FOCUS. In both the above situations, the results were different. Three things are very important for us to understand, to understand FOCUS. **Liking, Cause and Results or Outcomes**.

Liking

We must like what we do, or we must do what we like. In both the situations, liking is a must to have focus. Let's take the second case first. We must do what we like. What happens here, is very simple to understand. I like to watch movies and enjoy the same as I narrate it over to my friends. Here, my friends are my audience. The excitement which they show, while listening, gives a sense of satisfaction and a sense of happiness, that I have seen the movie, and I am the one or possibly the only one who knows the story. That is a child's mind. Still, it caters all aspects of focus. Therefore, if you like something, then your focus is just automatic. You will have great results. So, find what you like and do it.

There are situations when we do not have an option but still do it. We do not have a choice, and we do not like, but must do it. This is a space where majority of us get stuck. In my above first example, I might not like to study but must do. Many of us do not like the job that we do but must do it. There are people who work with bosses, and are unhappy, but no choice they must do. Why is this must do coming? The reason is simple. We do not possibly have an immediate choice to take a call. So, in this case, get your CAUSE in. Let us understand CAUSE.

Cause

Cause always has the biggest priority in everything. We do everything for a cause. There must be a reason behind everything that we do. Now, if we do not like a particular work, then our FOCUS will be less towards that work. The moment we add a pretext to it, it goes above liking and then we FOCUS. We most of the time do it unknowingly. For example, when we do a job which we possibly do not like, but we do it to earn our livelihood, for our family, then livelihood becomes a cause. To earn the bread and butter, is above liking the job, but with this cause, we have even better liking at this level. Therefore, whenever we do not like something, let us seek the cause to do it. Also, the cause has to be right or selfless. Then only, it will go beyond liking. The cause here is earn the living for the family and which is right and selfless. Now, what is the bread and butter, or earning the living? It is the outcome or the result.

Outcome or Result

Some of us are driven by the final outcomes. When you ask an athlete, what is your aim as an athlete. He will possibly say to earn a gold medal for his country. Nothing less than this would do for him or her. This earning of a gold is the result. Similarly, earning a living is the outcome, which is different, as a reason or a liking. The FOCUS here is on getting the gold. Getting the gold is the outcome. Results would always have a cause. Results always will give a sense of gratification. Gratification is beyond everything. We all somehow have these three within. Every right result or outcome, where we give back to the society, gives a sense of gratification. This is the finishing line where we get to. Results alone can be the big reason to focus.

Remember: F O C U S.... can be something like this.

F- *Find*; **O-** *Out*; **C-** *Cause*; **U-** *Until*; **S-** *Satisfied*;

CHAPTER-39
TOO MUCH....

"Too much"....as you speak it out, it will always give you a sense of being over full. This is too much to handle, we say, when we are burdened with work. If we do things too much, there is always a certain repercussion to it.

Once it happened.... This babumoshai (as often Bengalis in India are addressed), was getting married to a beautiful lady. Bengalis a fond of one sweet. Much not to guess out, it is the ROSSOGOLLA. ROSSO means a sweet thick juice, and GOLLA is a round shape sponge like cheese ball, which holds the sweet juice within. When you take a bite, the entire juice fills up your mouth with sweetness. So, the marriage feast had lot many items of food and to add on the sweet, it was the ROSSOGOLLA, which was going to be the showstopper, for the served menu.

Now, this babumoshai, who was going to be the jamaibabu (groom), had a hard resistance towards eating rossogolla and was very fond of this sweet. Now, this word TOO MUCH, came in between him and rossogolla. He was fond of this and had too many of them. Due to which he fell sick. Then his about to be wife, came to him and enquired about his well-being and tried to understand his possibility towards getting married that very evening. While enquiring, she came closer to his years and with a bit of anger, she said... "you are just TOO MUCH, let me get married once, then I shall see to it how you eat so many rossogollas". Now, see, this too much has, too many side effects.

Talking Too Much

When we talk too much, we shall always exaggerate. When we exaggerate, we often expose ourselves. The possibility to lie will always be high when we exaggerate. The more we lie, the more we lose our credentials. So, we must know how much to talk and when is it required to talk. The better way is to listen more, then talk, though seldom we do this.

Trusting Too Much

When we trust too much, we shall always have the probability to get betrayed. Trust again is something, which we should do with an understanding. Generally, trust is always blind. Still, there has to be a self-understanding on how much to trust anyone. The basic approach should be to reduce the possibility of getting betrayed. Once anyone gets betrayed, then everything is lost and repercussions can be really bad. Betrayal leads to destruction, revenge and massacres. History stands with its proof, that betrayals have seen the greatest of wars and bloodbaths.

So, too much of everything is bad.

When one loves someone too much, it shall make one weak.

When one fears too much, one shall always lose the faith in doing things.

When one eats too much, one can fall sick.

When one sleeps too much, one shall miss out to fulfil fill the dreams.

When one cares too much, one shall be taken for granted.

When one depends on others too much, one shall never be independent.

Remember : Too many cooks, spoils the broth.... so lets do that much what is required to be done. Energy is very important and should be used wisely.

CHAPTER-40
LET GO....

Life is always about fulfilment. We always look towards that whole pie of satisfaction and happiness. No one wants to be sad or dissatisfied. We always aspire for better, from wherever we stand. As we aspire, we thrive towards achieving. As we achieve, we develop a sense of possession. When we develop this sense, it is hard for us to live without it. Even the smallest of things we have achieved in life, we stamp it to be ours. This possession does often lead to sense of worry or fear of losing it.

Now this question comes, when we aspire to achieve, and after putting in a lot of effort, even if we achieve, then why are we not happy or satisfied, rather worry on losing it. That is how Bhagwat Gita profoundly mentions, *what was someone else's yesterday, is yours today and will be someone's tomorrow.* Happiness is possibly not in holding it, rather happiness is when we give it....let go is a beautiful concept.

Sense Of Easiness

Let go....let it be....lets leave it.....few of these lines, I am sure we must have come across at least once in our life. Either someone told us or at times it must have come from within. Then, whenever it has happened, it has created a sense of easiness always. Someone could have let gone a debate, which had been bothersome for one to keep holding it with some heated discussions. Ideally, no one wins a debate. As you let go it, you win it. Although the person who kept the discussions on, can things the other way, but it hardly matters. Also letting go, is very subjective to oneself. It can vary from people to people.

The Funny One

So, it happened as one of my friends had three girlfriends at a point in time, when he was in college. Initially, he used to boast for what he has, and we used to envy his possessions. Dating three beautiful girls and none of them new about the other, was something, which set him apart from other boys. He handled it classically. All the three were devoted, this is what he used to think. As friends, we used to say that you should hold one and let the other two go. He would never agree to it. Things were going very smoothly, until one day, he came to know that all three of his girlfriends had other boyfriends as well. Now, things were surprising for him. What, he thought he was smart at, he came to know that others were smatter than him. Nothing much could be done and with only one choice left with him was to let go. At that point in time, he was upset, but easy in his mind when he let them go. Now, he is a happily married man with two beautiful children.

The Classic Approach

Letting go also has a classical approach towards life. What we have achieved has been achieved. This is more of materialistic collections of our life, that I am mentioning. Now, when we leave it and move on, we have other things to achieve. Everyone can't achieve everything, but what we achieve is always with a purpose from the mother nature. It has a purpose in giving for whatever we think is by the virtue of our efficiency or efforts. Yes, without effort, nothing is possible, but what we hold, is always for a reason. It's very simple to understand, if we want to. Whatever, we have got today, will be of someone else tomorrow. It must go, but the thing is, are we readily giving it away is the question? For example, every knowledge that one gathers over the time, must share with others in every way he or she can. This is what let go means. Knowledge has come to one with a purpose to share and not to hold back. When we share knowledge, we feel happy and satisfied.

Awards, once received, should be done and dusted. One football match will never ever repeat itself. If the world champion in a chess world championship claimed the title of the grand master, can never repeat the same situation ever. It's a memory now. If he must win it again, he has to let go whatever he has achieved. Next time, the day of contest will be different, the opponent will be different, possibly the country of tournament will be different. Now, to win, one has to let go what was achieved, and prepare as per the upcoming contest. The more we hold on to the past achievement, the less shall become the possibility to win in the future. Sometimes holding on, does more damages than letting go.

Mind is an unresolved mystery. It has its ways to tell us what one must do. We sometimes read it rightly and sometimes do not. It gives us every possible way to understand what is simple and how can we remain happy and satisfied. Few things which we let go shall make a big difference in our life.

Let go EGO

Let go ANGER

Let go SELFISHNESS

Let go JEALOUSY

Let go ACHIEVEMENTS

Remember: At times just let go things, the tighter you hold, the less shall you have.

CHAPTER-41
THINKING LATERALLY

"THINK OVER IT.... ONCE AGAIN, BEFORE YOU TAKE THIS STEP".

We all must have heard it many times from people in and around us. When we think again, things get stuck. Stuck up so badly, that it never happens.

So, once it happened that, Mr. Dido, who was working for a clothing organization, wanted to do something on his own. Every morning, he would get up and this insect of self-establishment of making his own business would bite him. He had spent a good 15 years, in the clothing industry, and now he felt it was the right time to do something for himself. It was not easy to shift from employee mindset to employer mindset. To make sure that his decision was possibly a right one he would ask his wife, " Dear, was thinking, if I can do something on my own, what do you advice?", and, she would say... "see to it that you can do it, think over it again, doing business is never easy, I know Mr. Redder, failing miserably, who wanted to do his own business". He also, used to ask his friends and everyone used to say.... "think over it again". So, there was never a second thought that, Mr. Dido got. He could only get to say a no to himself and shelved the idea back.

Now, let's think a bit different. This same Mr. Dido decided that he would start off something on his own after spending some good time to his job. He went to his wife and said, "Dear, wanted to share something with you, I have planned to quit my job and start something in clothing. Yes, you need not to worry, I have my plans intact, and my things are absolutely in place. Also, there would be some challenges, in the beginning, but later down, with all your support, we should do great. If in case I fail, which I can, and I have failed many times in my job as well, but came up stronger every time. In that case also, will figure out something. Lets get along quickly."

In both the cases, the approach towards the thinking of Mr. Dido, needs to be observed. In both the cases, he wanted to do the business, but the way he put things in front of his wife, mattered. This is what we call as *lateral thinking*. It is not what we present, rather it is, how we present what we present, and without a creative thinking, this will never be possible. Lateral thinking is a problem-solving approach, which involves looking at any problem with solutions. It's more of looking at every problem or challenge with a reason to solve it. It is more of a step wise reasoning, which promotes the creative self of people.

Be Solution Oriented

The first thing, is one has to look for solutions every time. Every problem, has a solution. We sometimes get stuck so much within the problem, that we overlook the solutions. All problems that is coming to us, must have some way out and when we look into those problems, with a way out, then it becomes easier and interesting to solve the problem. Also, if a problem, stays unresolved, it still teaches us to handle it. Every problem, coming our way has a purpose and it is up to us how we look at it.

Past Experiences

Creativity, is nothing but amalgamation of our past experiences. In one of my training sessions, where I was an attendee, we were given a chess board 10 ft by 10ft flex. Five people each in one team. Every team was given some props like a dice, cone caps, cones etc. Now the interesting part comes. We were told to create a game with this flex and the props. All the teams got really engrossed and created some fantastic interesting games out of the blue. One team created a game and named it cricket on chess. Another team created another game and called it as the blind walkers on chess board. So they would put the props on the board and tie up the eyes with a piece of cloth and would ask the participant to walk on the board. Now, when you see the creativity, you will find all these games that are created are from our past experience. That is how, every experience that we go through in life teaches us something. The more we are solution oriented, the better we use these for our creative self. Even if we fail, doesn't matter, we at least carry an experience with us, and experience is everything. So in lateral thinking, we can use our past experiences.

Feedbacks

Life is never partial. It gives a fair chance to everyone. To have a creative mind, we must seek feedbacks. Feedbacks, again have a big challenge. If you are asking for feedbacks from people, then be rest assured, you will get the unwanted ones as well. They will be good and bad both, and even the biased ones. Filtering becomes very difficult at this point. Therefore, the best thing is to get the feedbacks, without making it an agenda to ask for it.

Once it happened so, that I was delivering a workshop on communications for some banking employees. This was a leading bank in India. For me, this project was a crucial one, as this was the first time, I got an opportunity from banking sector. I had been into sales and product industry. This was something new and challenging . So, it mattered a lot to me. Anyways, the session went off very well by the grace of God. I was happy, still was looking for some areas, where I found something more could have been done. Now this is always with me, that next time, something better can be done. This room for improvement, helps me to come out with some innovative and interesting ideas always. Here, rather than asking them, how did they find the session and what all things do I need to do for them next time, I put them a question.... on what all topics do they want to learn more in my sessions. This was a very different way to put, and all credits goes to my mentor Dr. Rajan, who taught me this. So seeking feedbacks and implementing them is another way to grow your lateral thinking abilities.

Remember: As we grow up every day, so does our thinking. The more we give our creative self a chance, the better shall we think laterally.

CHAPTER-42
UNPLUGGED

UNPLUGGED....is very simple to understand. To most of us, it is, any electric device not connected to the plug point from where the current flows. When current does not flow, it is in a state of rest. No action happens.

Science would have a lot of its understanding to this. To us the understanding could vary. Now imagine a jiffy steamer, inside a readymade clothing showroom, kept unplugged for a long time at the corner of the trial room or the stock room, would give the impression that either it's of no use or it is no more required. Same jiffy, if kept for its own sale inside any electronic shop, the value is worth it. Now, at both places, this jiffy is unplugged, but the perceived value differs. This word "unplugged" is a simple yet strong state of positioning. The value changes from place to place.

We human beings believe life is action and getting into action is what it is all about. This certainly is. The dynamics of life is to keep moving. There is a definite dichotomy to this thought. When we are continuously into action, how and when should we think which action is to be taken? This break in action and then think over what is to be done and then again getting back to action, is finely called as being UNPLUGGED. Very similar to the jiffy example above. When we are continuously performing, the same thing again and again our perceived value goes down. This is a for granted situation for people in and around us. Be it being an employee or into self-owned business, we need to get reconnected and rejuvenated, renewed and restarted.

Self-Evaluation

So once upon a time, there lived a guy, Sam. Sam was an employee to an office which manufactured biscuits. He had elongated his job for good time with this office. Nothing interesting was happening with Sammy. Same getting up in the morning, making his breakfast, living alone, going to work, coming back and then the same routine again and again. No increment, no recognition, in fact, his bonus was also less in comparison to others, as his superior stated, that there was not much need for him as he was all alone. Sam, was not happy and people in and around could feel it.

Then, what happened, was a surprise for all to know. Sammy dear went absconding for few days. Ok, one think was important to mention. Sam's primary work was to serve tea and coffee to all the workers. In fact, the owner's entire lunch and other hospitality of guests were also taken care by Sam only. He was so good at his work, that he would rightly know, what is to be given to whom at what time. So, if one day Sam was not available, this office went mad. The work really got impacted and now, he was absconding. There were replacements hunted, some of employees even, went to the nearby offices and asked, if someone could be found with a better payout. Few people were made to join, but things did not work out. Then one fine morning, the entire office got surprised, when they saw their Sammy dear walking towards them with the tea tray, and he had a smile. People naturally asked him, where had he been. To this Sam replied, " I had taken a break from my work. This break made me realize, that I must be valued to my own self first, then only others would understand my significance. I got married, and understood, my wife respects me a lot and I am everything to her. Then when I came back, I met the owner of our company. He was very happy to see me. He immediately asked me to join and gave me a salary hike and the pending bonuses."

Understanding One's Worth

The connotation of being unplugged is not shirking away from assigned responsibilities, rather it is understanding once own worth. By unplugged we can understand to disconnect. This disconnect is with a meaning. Disconnecting can be every day, once a month, or even once in six months or so on, where you give sometime to yourself to introspect. One must mull over, on one's own actions. Now, to contemplate over self, one need to stop what one is doing. This break is very important for self-growth. This break can be and should be as per one's own convenience. There are definite perks on being unplugged.

This **improves the productivity** of whatever one is doing.

The **focus** towards the work gets increased.

One can understand, his or her **own value** and can accordingly, do what he or she things right.

The **creative self** gets a boost in every individual. The hobbies that one had in the past years, comes back with an impact of maturity and an option towards livelihood. Many people have made their hobbies their profession. This could only have been done, when they got unplugged from their existing work.

Unplugged approach provides a unique ability to **solve problems**. When we disconnect and then again reconnect, we come up with solutions.

Most importantly, it lets us know how to **manage** the odd situations, which helps in **releasing stress** and makes our **physical health** better.

Remember: A field that has rested a while, gives a plentiful crop.

CHAPTER-43
I-QUIT

There goes a proverb... *"Winners never quit, and quitters never wins"*.

Either you win or lose, does not really matter. All that shall matter, is you being there till the finish. The finish line is always the factor. Just imagine or go back to your past experiences and try to remember that one finishing line, which you had touched. Does not matter, you were topping the chart, or your name was below down the list. All that must have mattered was, reaching the finishing line. The glory is in completing, and not in quitting. It could be in any field, be it athletics, academics or stage.

The Habit

If quitting is a habit, then not quitting is also a habit. We develop both the habits at our very tender age. The circumstances play a very important role in the development of both these habits. As a child, I was in a boarding school. This was very clear from the primary wing itself, that we are on our own and shall have to manage self in a very disciplined way. So, if we were to make up our bed post we woke up, then, it was never a choice for us to leave it undone. Now, it has become a habit, not to leave the bed unfinished, once I wake up. If in case I keep it undone, it seems some work is incomplete. Today, this has become a routine. The next very important thing to note is, for quitting something, we don't need to seek permission from anyone other than our own self. As and when we develop a mindset to give up on anything, we call it a quit. So, quit is more of a function of our mind set. Let us dig a bit down, to understand what makes us quit and if we know the reason can we work on it ?

Urge to Grow

Strange but true. When we want to grow in life, most of the time we leave it mid-way. The urge to grow is always there, but the efforts that is required to grow in life, is often not seen in people. Stagnation is death and growth is life. In between this, somewhere lies the possibility of quitting. This quitting here is from the commitments or may be from the right things required to grow. As soon as people, come across any challenge, in the journey of growth, most of them quit. Those who do not, make the history. It is just about being there. The goal of growth should be so big, that quit, will be never an option in existence.

Bridge of Comfort to Discomfort

No one likes discomfort, and this is to humans. If we observe animals, they thrive to live. Nothing comes easy to them. That's how nature is. If we want to have something special, then we shall have to move out of our comfort zone and move ahead to achieve it. In fact, if we go to any of our past achievements, we will observe, that all achievements needed that extraordinary effort. For every reward, there were those sweating days or sleepless nights, which made us reach where we wanted to be. All changes that happen in nature, is about discomfort and that must be adopted, with no choice left. The best way to fight discomfort, is to accept it and work accordingly. Gradually, it becomes a part of us, and the journey of life continues and along the path, we accomplish many goals, which we later realize in life. As and when we comprehend those accomplishments, we feel good and satisfied. So, discomfort is the only, comfort, which we embrace and realize much later in our life.

Fear to fail

Most of us are not taught to fail or handle failures. Rest assured, we all have either or will fail in our lifetime. We fail, when we attempt and when we attempt, then only we shall succeed. As parents or teachers, we must make our children understand how to handle failures. The fear is injected inside us from a very young age in life. As a result of which, the moment, we see failure approaching, we blame the situation and quit. This blaming is either through us or even through our loved once, when they sympathize us, by saying… "now worries, it happens, possibly you were not meant for it. Forget it and do something else". I believe if we fail in something, then it is a sure shot success which is not too far. The only thing is, how many attempts are we ready to put, and get that success instead of quitting. It is just about, the number of attempts and failing one more time. Finally, after failing so many times, we will get bored and get through, but never quit. Failing is learning.

Quitting is always a pattern, which the mind reinforces as a human behaviour. If we want to quit, then, there are some things with us and not much of requirement for our personal or professional growth, can be put in auction.

1. Let us quit the habit of indiscipline.
2. Let us quit anger.
3. Let us quit ego.
4. Let us quit those habits which are not good for our health.
5. Let us quit hatred.
6. Let us quit, jealousy.
7. last but not the least, let us quit the habit of quitting.

Remember: Those who win never quit, and those who quit can never win.

www.ingramcontent.com/pod-product-compliance
Lightning Source LLC
LaVergne TN
LVHW061545070526
838199LV00077B/6903